Cambridge

Elements in Translat
edite
Kirsten Malmkjær
University of Leicester
Sabine Braun
University of Surrey

ON-SCREEN LANGUAGE IN VIDEO GAMES

A Translation Perspective

Mikołaj Deckert
University of Lodz
Krzysztof Hejduk
University of Lodz

CAMBRIDGE
UNIVERSITY PRESS

Shaftesbury Road, Cambridge CB2 8EA, United Kingdom

One Liberty Plaza, 20th Floor, New York, NY 10006, USA

477 Williamstown Road, Port Melbourne, VIC 3207, Australia

314–321, 3rd Floor, Plot 3, Splendor Forum, Jasola District Centre, New Delhi – 110025, India

103 Penang Road, #05–06/07, Visioncrest Commercial, Singapore 238467

Cambridge University Press is part of Cambridge University Press & Assessment, a department of the University of Cambridge.

We share the University's mission to contribute to society through the pursuit of education, learning and research at the highest international levels of excellence.

www.cambridge.org
Information on this title: www.cambridge.org/9781009045513

DOI: 10.1017/9781009042321

First published 2022

A catalogue record for this publication is available from the British Library.

ISBN 978-1-009-04551-3 Paperback
ISSN 2633-6480 (online)
ISSN 2633-6472 (print)

On-Screen Language in Video Games

A Translation Perspective

Elements in Translation and Interpreting

DOI: 10.1017/9781009042321
First published online: October 2022

Mikołaj Deckert
University of Lodz

Krzysztof Hejduk
University of Lodz

Author for correspondence: Mikołaj Deckert, mikolaj.deckert@uni.lodz.pl

Abstract: In this Element, the authors focus on the translational dimension of 'on-screen language' (OSL). They analyse a data set covering the Polish localisations of *Tom Clancy's The Division 2* and *Shadow Warrior 2*, from which over 1000 cases of unique and meaningful OSL were extracted, almost exclusively in languages other than Polish. Close to 100 representative examples are examined in this Element to map out a comprehensive typological account of OSL. First, visual-verbal stimuli are categorised by their prominence in the 3D environment. The second typology focuses on the identified OSL functions. A supplementary typological distinction is proposed based on the technical (*static vs. dynamic*) implementation of OSL. The discussion of findings and implications notably comprises input from an interview that the authors conduced with a lead level developer behind *Shadow Warrior 2* to provide a complementary professional perspective on OSL and its translation.

Keywords: video games, on-screen language, interlingual translation, visual–verbal stimuli, localising textures

ISBNs: 9781009045513 (PB), 9781009042321 (OC)
ISSNs: 2633-6480 (online), 2633-6472 (print)

Contents

Introduction

In this Element, we concentrate on the allocation of visual attention in video games from a cross-linguistic and cross-cultural perspective. Our postulate is that there can exist remarkable and yet unexplored mismatches between the experiences of a player who speaks the game's source language (SL) and a player who relies exclusively on the target language (TL) version of the localised game. More specifically, this Element deals with a subset of attention allocation cases where the structure that is an object of attention for the player is linguistic in nature – it is accessed by them reading a text. We then further narrow down the scope by starting from the premise that these structures vary in terms of *prominence*. Some of them are more prototypically salient than others, which means they are easier to visually identify and more likely to be interpreted as relevant. At the other end of the spectrum, there are elements with liminal prominence. Whether salient or not, these elements have different functions and rely on different mechanisms, which can pose challenges in interlingual translation.

In the first part of the Element, we contextualise the research by talking about multiple facets of video games (VGs) and outlining the constructs pertinent to on-screen language (OSL) with reference to findings from cognitive psychology as well as research into film translation. Then, in the second and third parts, we demonstrate how analogous elements function in VGs, with data sourced from *Tom Clancy's The Division 2* (*TCTD2*), developed by Massive Entertainment (owned by Ubisoft), and *Shadow Warrior 2* (*SW2*), developed by the Flying Wild Hog, then an independent studio. Based on the qualitative analysis, we propose a primarily two-pronged typology. First, cases of OSL are showed to differ in terms of their cognitive status: how prominent they are and how likely they are to be accessed by players. Second, they are found to vary functionally, which is motivated by several dimensions that will be discussed. The typology can then be complemented by incorporating the technical parameters of how OSL is implemented into the game. The analysis is positioned against insights from an interview with a professional game creator working for Flying Wild Hog, which discusses how OSL is frequently deployed and can be carefully designed, and thus significant to the player's meaning-making processes. Critically, our emphasis is on the challenges that these elements create for localisation, especially their implications for receptor experience across languages and cultures. The rationale behind this publication is therefore to gain a better understanding of OSL in VGs as a critical step in minimising interlingual and cross-cultural meaning construction asymmetries.

VIDEO GAMES: THE POTENTIAL FOR ON-SCREEN LANGUAGE AND TRANSLATION

1 On-Screen Language: From Films to Video Games

When thinking of games as products to be translated, one has to consider their complex semiotic set-up. Bernal-Merino (2020: 299) emphasises this premise, saying that '[a] video game is not a text, although some can contain millions of words. A video game is a digital machine made up of hardware and software that generates polysemiotic virtual experiences.'

Following from that idea, this Element's central construct is that of attention, or more precisely visual attention. An imperative characteristic of visual attention – and also our guiding idea – will be that it is a limited resource: 'at any given time only a small amount of the information available on the retina can be processed and used' (Desimone & Duncan, 1995: 193). A complementary quality is that attention is selective – with the vast array of stimuli around us, we allocate attention to some and do not attend to others (see Section 9.2 for a more detailed discussion).

The specific mechanism we examine is labelled 'on-screen language' (OSL), or visual–verbal components of products such as feature films, series, clips and VGs. 'Visual' refers to the way in which information is coded in audiovisual material, thus drawing a dividing line between input that is registered visually and aurally. The data is then 'verbal' in the sense that it is coded through language, as opposed to cases where the visual elements rely on non-linguistic signs. A further relevant differentiation is between 'diegetic' and 'non-diegetic' on-screen elements (Matamala & Orero, 2015). The former function within the plot while the latter are explicitly superimposed as the product is edited. The screenshot in Figure 1 illustrates cases of both diegetic and non-diegetic text. The inscription on the banner or the public transport display is diegetic while other information, for example, about the distance from 'Narodowe Muzeum Historii Amerykańskiej' (National Museum of American History) being '0.3 km' away (in the upper left-hand corner) is non-diegetic.

We are primarily interested in the diegetic type. The rationale behind this choice is that the cognitive and communicative status of non-diegetic text on screen is unambiguous compared to the status of diegetic text. In this analysis we wish to specifically address the issue of OSL's status by starting from the premise that stimuli vary in terms of how likely they are to draw attention to themselves. While some stimuli will be more or less prototypically prominent, some will move away from prototypicality, approaching what we term 'liminality', whereby prominence is here understood in line with its formulation as a parameter of construal in cognitive linguistics (cf. Langacker, 2008, 2007)

Figure 1 Diegetic and non-diegetic texts in *Tom Clancy's The Division 2*

where the term 'salience' has also been widely used (cf. Tomlin & Myachykov, 2015). Liminally prominent stimuli are those that can still be accessed by receptors, but the likelihood of doing so is not as high as it would be with prototypically prominent instances. The continuum ranging from the prototypical to the liminal will be discussed in more detail in Section 5. On a conceptual-terminological note, while for ease of exposition throughout this Element we consistently refer to 'prominence' of OSL, a notion very much related to prominence – or its constitutive facet – is that of 'ostensiveness', which can be defined in line with Sperber and Wilson's (1995) idea that ostensive stimuli trigger the presumption that they are relevant enough for the receptor to deserve the receptor's attention.

So far, a limited amount of work has been devoted to these or similar phenomena, primarily in the area of audiovisual translation and media accessibility. Matamala and Orero (2015) talk about 'text on screen' in the context of audio description, an accessibility service that can be conceived of as intersemiotic translation, while Deckert and Jaszczyk (2019) and Deckert (2021) investigated it in the context of interlingual film translation, with the latter paper only briefly alluding to VGs.

Specifically with reference to VGs, a complex typology of 'narrative oriented game text' considering 'text function and translation priorities' developed by

O'Hagan and Mangiron (2013) includes the category 'art assets, printed materials and other online/screen materials', which rather neatly matches the construct of diegetic OSL. However, given the more general profile of O'Hagan and Mangiron's volume, that category of text is not discussed in greater detail by the authors, even though they give examples – such as posters, maps, signs and billboards (156, 162) – and suggest functions (see Section 9.1).

Bernal-Merino (2015: 130) moreover discusses the 'artwork with words' in the context of translation – a concept paramount to this Element's analysis of visual–verbal components – which he describes as something more general than OSL: as part of the packaging, merchandising, the user interface, or the in-game graphic textures. Another term, 'graphic-embedded text', is then also used by Bernal-Merino in the context of the need for multi-layered graphic file format to 'be able to edit the text neatly without altering the original art style' (see Section 9.3.2), exemplified by 'linguistic graphic art in game textures' of *Escape from Monkey Island* (2000) localised from English into Spanish (130). Graphic-embedded text, which is said to, among other things, contribute to the credibility of the game-world, 'may appear anywhere in a game, regardless of the genre, and it certainly requires translation in order to keep players engrossed in the adventure and not to alienate them with texts in languages that are not required by the story' (Bernal-Merino, 2015: 130–1). Bernal-Merino also recognises that 'translation of information conveyed graphically ... with meaningful cultural and linguistic relevance' is one of 'the most common challenges shared between audiovisual and multimedia productions' (65). He illustrates this with a case of what we name OSL left untranslated in a Spanish version of an originally English-language game, moreover commenting that:

> [L]ocalising graphic information is not only time-consuming and expensive; graphics in video games can be easily missed out when translating because this text is stored in an image format within a graphics folder, and it can only be edited with graphic editing software. If game developers do not have a strategy in place to name and process translatable strings stored as graphic files, they are likely to be forgotten during the translation process and be left in the original language in all the localised versions of the game.
> (Bernal-Merino, 2015: 65; cf. Bernal-Merino, 2013: 182–3)

We attempt to build on these fundamental claims as well as Bernal-Merino's (2015: 67) usage of the term '*on-screen*' in the context of voicing over 'on-screen *signs*' – by an extra-diegetic narrator, in contrast to the remastering of filmic graphics – demonstrating that greater recognition of the potential behind meaningful OSL could benefit the processes of game localisation, the quality of the products, or even their development.

We interviewed Michał Mazur, a game development team representative and the lead level designer for the *SW2* game, about the phenomena investigated in this Element, and will be integrating his input into the relevant segments of discussion for an additional insider's perspective. The interview was conducted in Polish, transcribed and translated into English.

2 Video Games as a Medium and More Than That

2.1 The Economic Context: Popularity of Gaming

The official website of the US International Trade Administration states that the global gaming industry was 'valued at $159.3 billion in 2020, with 2.7 billion gamers worldwide' and that statistically '75% of US households have at least one gamer' (International Trade Administration, n.d.). By comparison, the media and entertainment industry – which includes VGs – is valued at '$660 billion ... enduring an estimated $53B or 7.3% decline due to the pandemic' (International Trade Administration, 2020). In contrast, however, they report that globally, 'the impact from the pandemic has driven sales [of VGs], with the U.S. seeing a record 31% increase in consumer spending on video gaming and subscription services' as well as over 13 per cent growth in 2020 mobile gaming revenue, to 77.2 billion dollars. Furthermore, they state that '80% of U.S. gaming companies are looking abroad to expand sales'. The popularity of esports is also mentioned, with their projected growth 'estimated to surpass $2.5 billion by 2024'. In the context of competitive gaming spectacles, the Polish National Agency for Academic Exchange (NAWA, 2020) reported that '[i]n 2020, e-sports are projected to enjoy viewership of more than 70 million people for final matches. That's more viewers than the NBA finals, NHL Stanley Cup finals or the World Series'. They also uphold that 'almost a third of people on this planet are gamers [who play routinely]' and that '1.2 billion play on a PC'. Games are an object of globally operating[1] businesses, both high-budget and independent ones. They are made by professionals as well as amateurs. More broadly, VGs can be seen as a new, growing[2] industry that is 'important politically and economically' (Wong, 2011: 3).

---

[1] Before it reached the contemporary, global Internet state, it is significant to mention that Japan, the United States and the United Kingdom (Izushi & Aoyama, 2006) were considered particularly major hotspots for its rapid market development.

[2] Bernal-Merino points out that the interest in gaming is on the rise across gender and age groups, citing substantial average playtime a week: '[t]he growth is due to three main factors: the ubiquity of highly capable portable devices, the availability of a wide array multimedia interactive of entertainment software in multiple languages, and the demand for 1st person experiences in new media' (Bernal-Merino, 2018 as cited in Bernal-Merino, 2020: 297).

2.2 The Socio-Cultural Context

2.2.1 Inclusivity and Accessibility

The US National Library Service for the Blind and Print Disabled website (NLS, 2015) recognises gaming's potential to 'boost creativity, improve problem-solving skills, and cultivate teamwork', while also highlighting some of the resources that have been made available for gamers with disabilities. These resources include: modified controllers, audio adaptations for people with visual impairment and expert accessibility reviews of new games, among a list with almost fifty items at the time of writing. Despite that, the list is said to still not be comprehensive, which gives credence the idea that outside resources for the medium are being developed, yet are fragmented (cf. Bernal-Merino, 2020: 306–8). However, games might be becoming more accessible in a different sense, too.

Lipkin (2019) explains that there are 'significant motivations that drive independent game developers to create games in spite of worsening economic conditions', further using the term 'the Indiepocalypse' (an amalgamation of apocalypse and the 'indie' scene – independent media development) to refer to 'the result of a predisposition towards creativity matched with technological innovations and structural conditions that make independent commercial game development faster, easier, and more accessible'. Although this points to specific problems of that scene, it also showcases the democratisation of tools and assets for VG production.

Pluralisation of Content

Fisher and Harvey (2013: 1) specify that in gaming 'there are successful models in which we can observe other, more inclusive, modes of welcoming previously marginalized and excluded groups ... . The demographic landscape of this culture is radically changing, particularly in terms of age and gender.' This could indicate pluralistic demographic segments capable of appreciating the potential for an equally diversified supply of game productions manufactured by different groups of people. It corresponds, at least partially, with the opinion of Keogh (2018: 14), who observes that:

> [H]obbyists, amateurs, students, and artists ... are pushing videogame development in new directions in terms of aesthetics, design process, and distribution channels. ... [The industry] transitioned from a period of aggressive formalisation through the 1980s to the early 2000s into a more intense intermingling of formal and informal actors and processes in the early 2010s.

What is more, assuming that diversity and inclusivity can function interdependently, all this may contribute to the conception that joining gaming social circles is not a difficult feat, asserting the subculture's accessibility in its broadest sense. Yet for that, independently developed games are only a portion of the wider cultural landscape, as Keogh (2018: 14) proclaims: '[n]ew audiences, distribution platforms, and development tools are expanding the videogame industry into an ecosystem that is at once broadly global and intensely localised'.

Heterogeneity of Gaming Communities

Gaming subcultures can be seen as quite multifarious. The advent of social media brought about local and macro-cultural digital ludic promotion, gaming wikis, dedicated forums, together with preservationism, game archives, new ways for LARPing (live action role-playing) or classic table-top gaming, the sharing of cosplay (costume play) along with casemodding (modifying or tuning the computer's chassis) and aesthetician computer tune-up photography, story analysis and plot discussions, as well as the production of fan art and fan fiction in 'casual' or 'hardcore' fandoms (communities sharing interest in the same series).

Moreover, the emergence of esports, competitive and/or charitable gamejamming (a type of tech-skill demo or game development, restrained by specific conditions; cf. Kultima, 2021) and speedrunning (gaining records in games as fast as possible), machinima (cinematography utilising, for example, game engines), game modification communities, such as Nexusmods.com, as well as other formations contingent to gaming culture diversified the way people play games and their reasons for playing. The sharing and distributing of 'amateur', 'homebrew' games, tech-skill demonstrations and other user-generated content particularly related to game making (cf. Young, 2018; Camper, 2005[3]) also contributed to this.

But aside from 'accessibility within' gaming, 'accessibility to' gaming is rapidly developing alongside. Chiefly, prospective players can easily find information online on the titles they wish to experience. This includes creations that could even be very niche. It is also relatively easy to find detailed, novice-friendly instructions for proper VG and hardware installation. Most importantly, though, the digital releases of VGs are overtaking physical ones on the global market.[4] This arguably makes it easier to acquire games, as well as their localisations,[5] whether official or fan-made. Assuming this, and the growing

---

[3] We wish to point out that these two sources are academic theses. Although that does not imply inferior quality, it highlights the scarcity of relevant publications and thus indicates some of the challenges of working with under-explored (or contentious) topics. As said by Jeff Vogel of Spiderweb Software during a 2018 Game Developers Conference, '[The film industry] is a far better understood industry than ours. Video games are young, nobody knows anything. We're still scrambling to figure out how do we design these things' (GDC, 2018b: 7:42–8:00).

[4] Analysts Michael J. Olson and Yung Kim estimated in a report for Piper Jaffray '[V]ideo games will be ~100% digital in the coming years, and while exact timing is hard to pinpoint, we think 2022 is a realistic expectation' (quoted in Palumbo, 2018).

[5] Assuming that localisation and media accessibility, in their broadest sense, help to enable as wide an audience as possible, regardless of their capabilities, to access the content of individual pieces of media as close to their original potential as possible – whatever that might mean case by case.

academic interest in VGs, one could advocate that the idea of a small, hermetic 'gaming-toy' culture is certain to be brushed off as a tired stereotype by today's standards.

2.3 Myths, Controversies, Anachronisms and Stereotypes

2.3.1 Demoralisation and Mature Themes

Although it may be true that '[l]ong gone are the days when hobbyist bedroom coders with access to digital computers and 'how to' articles of basic video game code, jump-started the formation of the video game industry' (Izushi & Aoyama, 2006, as cited in Wong, 2011: 1; cf. Wolf & Perron, 2003), such practices are still very present and becoming increasingly commonplace for enthusiasts. In short, '[t]oday video games ... are in practically all American households' (Amick et al., 2015: 1) and 'playing video games has by now become not only an acceptable leisure activity but also a popular one for people across the world' (Bernal-Merino, 2020: 297).

Despite this, there are still some controversies around the proliferation of games, which need to be thoroughly considered, as they pertain to health, safety and ethics. Alongside such vital, yet heated discussions like the hazards of VG consumption in the era of their popularisation, the question of research fragmentation and lack of clear scientific consensus in the findings is worth discussion. Ferguson and Colwell (2017: 321) suggested the following:

> [S]cholars disagree widely regarding video game influences and ... do not appear to be immune to the types of generational and experience effects that influence opinions in the general public. ... There are numerous possible causal chains that might explain links between discipline, negative attitudes toward youth, video game experience, and negative attitudes toward video games. Given that current data are correlational, no causal attributions can be made.

The notion that VGs as a medium are unsuitable for children or are fantasies for adult escapism has also been contradicted by statistical data from organisations such as the Interactive Software Federation of Europe, whose Pan-European Game Information (PEGI) system in 2020 rated 23 per cent of the products as adequate for children aged three, then 21 per cent and 27 per cent of them respectively for ages seven and twelve.[6] This, however, does not mean that there are no VGs directed at adults. It is quite the opposite. Some VGs tackle difficult or extensively philosophical topics – and many a time such games become cult classics. To touch on that aspect, Max Derrat, a YouTube creator

---

[6] This counterargument was put forward by Bernal-Merino in June 2021 during an online workshop at the School of Translation and Foreign Languages of The Hang Seng University of Hong Kong entitled 'New Translation Studies Challenges and New Job Profiles'.

advocating for the academic value of VGs alongside books, music, poetry and movies, opens his personal list of the 'Ten Most Profound Games Ever Made' hypothesising that 'some games . . . reach such a level of sophistication that they demand vigorous intellectual inquiry' (Derrat, 2018: 0:10–0:17).

2.3.2 Violence and Substance Abuse

In the aforementioned PEGI report, games from that period – even those allowed for children aged seven and twelve by PEGI – were also shown to be more likely to be rated as 'violent' than by any other content descriptor. Nonetheless, it is worth remembering that there will be differences when it comes to the kind and intensity of what could be broadly termed 'violence'. Moreover, when analysing such a complex issue as violence in video games, it may also be crucial to consider the context and intention behind the implementation of what can be considered 'violent' in media, on a case-by-case basis. Bernal-Merino (2020: 298) references the labelling of games as adequate for exposure to children (aged three to sixteen) *despite* such descriptors, ultimately claiming that 'the majority of games available are not violent or gory'.

Furthermore, a recent study by Turel (2020: 2) has found that 'the moral panic over [assaults and] video games is largely unsubstantiated, especially among light to moderate gamers'. Although not directly relating to violence,[7] this can be further substantiated by the findings on aggression produced by Ferguson and Wang (2019: 9), who posit that '[a] daily hour spent on M-rated video games would result in an increase of 0.022 in the measure of physical aggression. By this metric it would take 27 h/day of M-rated video game play to raise aggression to a clinically observable level.' On a related note, a piece titled 'Do Video Games Kill?' points out that 'focusing so heavily on video games, news reports downplay the broader social contexts' (Sternheimer, 2007: 14).

Others relate this concept to frustration more than to the virtual violence itself: Przybylyski and colleagues (2014: 455) found that the 'impedances of player competence satisfactions increase cognitive, affective, and behavioral aspects of aggression', and that 'these effects were wholly independent of violent game contents'. Psychological need-thwarting is not exclusive to gaming, but relates to a 'myriad ways across most life domains' (455). This invites comparisons with the issue of violence in other audiovisual media, such as television and cinema (cf. e.g. Bareither, 2020), but this would go beyond the scope of this Element.

---

[7] According to Sternheimer (2007: 15), 'Aggression includes a broad range of emotions and behaviors, and is not always synonymous with violence.'

Another point of contention is that VG consumption may correlate with escapism through narcotics. The conclusion of Turel and Bechara's (2019: 384) research into substance abuse is that 'light video gaming can be protective in terms of substance use, while too much video gaming is associated with increased substance use'. Moreover, the aforementioned report by PEGI only saw a small minority of games content-described with 'drugs/alcohol'[8] – none of which were targeted at children aged three to twelve.

All this suggests that the concerning phenomena of violence, hedonism and other, general cases of what might be named 'the corruption of children', if they happen to occur together with VG consumption at all, ultimately seem too multifaceted and multifactored as correlates to definitively conclude either way.

2.4 Potential and Utility

Contrary to some of the claims in the previous section, gaming is repeatedly portrayed as beneficial beyond recreation (cf. Gee, 2005). As Bavelier and colleagues (2012: 1) claim, 'Over the past few years, the very act of playing action video games has been shown to enhance several different aspects of visual selective attention. . . . [A]ction game players may allocate attentional resources more automatically, possibly allowing more efficient early filtering of irrelevant information.'[9] Accepting this, it may not be surprising that the potential of VGs have seen widespread use in niche contexts outside of entertainment.

2.4.1 Institutional Importance

Computer games, on top of building on a rich ludic history, see use in contexts such as training and simulation (Pursel & Stubbs, 2017: 277–95), education (Janarthanan, 2012), research (Bohannon, 2014; Lv et al., 2013; Khatib et al., 2011), activism (Whaley, 2015; Bogost, 2006), health and rehabilitation (Lieberman, 2012; Griffiths, 2005) and more.

Prominent sources like New York's Museum of Modern Art have recognised that at the least some VGs can be artistic. Then senior curator at the museums architecture and design department, Paola Antonelli (2012) said: 'Are video games art? They sure are, but they are also design.' However, it is not just art galleries and similar institutions that take interest in VGs: '[Games] are a major driving force in electronic innovation and development. Though you would hardly guess this from their modest beginning' (Amick et al., 2015: 1).

---

[8] An analogous report for 2019 appears to be unavailable, however the results from a similar report from 2017 have been comparable (Pan European Gaming Information, 2019).

[9] This point is further developed in Section 9.2.

Schooling and language-teaching is especially noteworthy. Shaffer and colleagues (2005: 105) attested to this in 2005, claiming that 'corporations, the government, and the military have already recognized and harnessed [VGs'] tremendous educative power'. Despite this, '[m]ost educators [were at that point] dismissive of video games' (105), which relates back to the question of controversies and stereotypes about gaming, posed in Section 2.3.

To stress another determining aspect of gaming in educational development, a recent study by deHaan (2019) suggests that language teaching and learning is possible with games at this stage and can further evolve 'by integrating important aspects of goal-setting ... and a broader consideration of games' (1). That is not to suggest that video games dedicated to personal growth are yet to be developed: 'educative' and 'serious' games can be said to date as far back as the popular *Oregon Trail* (1971). With that in mind, however, it seems essential to mention that the utilisation of educational games has not always been optimal: '[s]erious game designers are conflicted by contradictions between educational environments and entertainment environments' (Sanford et al., 2015: 104).

2.5 The Medial Context

2.5.1 Gaming Turning Mainstream

As a global multi-million dollar entertainment industry, a stimulus for technological innovation (Amick et al., 2015: 1), a stable source of professional opportunities in game development and localisation (cf. Dunne, 2006: 121–34), and with its formally recognised potential to be a unique form of art consumption (Antonelli, 2012; Gee, 2006), gaming has not only become a popular, global hobby (Bernal-Merino, 2020: 297–312), but perhaps a burgeoning mainstream phenomenon. With researchers examining their beneficial uses, as well as any possibility of harm[10] (and, consequently, responses to mitigate or neutralise that – going as far as stimulating changes to legislative and regulatory systems[11]), it has

---

[10] This Element attempts to outline the main ones, following Uysal's (2017: 178) opinion on this matter: 'The most important risks or harmful effects are internet and computer games addiction, violence, loss of identity and lack of communication.' Harvey and Fisher (2014: 576) raise a related issue of inclusivity observing that 'articulations of post-feminism within the digital game industry provide insights into the tensions inherent in introducing action for change within a conservative culture of production, particularly for women in the industry'.

[11] Although they remain controversial, and their effectiveness is disputed: Dillio (2014: 110) evaluates that 'the usage of social scientific research by legislatures to censor video games has been unpersuasive and a failure in almost every attempt', while Copenhaver (2014: 170) links several issues relating to this notion: '[Brown v. Entertainment Merchants Association] Supreme Court decision ... found violent video games do not cause minors to be aggressive, nor can violent video games be regulated. ... Using Goffman's dramaturgical analysis, the violent video game pseudo-agenda is seen as frontstage, while governmental economic interest in video game software companies is seen as backstage.'

become difficult not to recognise that VGs contribute and relate to a vast array of different social spheres beyond recreation and entertainment.

2.5.2 Defining Characteristics of the Medium

Contemporary VGs are greatly heterogeneous and interrelated with sociocultural spheres outside of pure entertainment. Because of that, adequately defining VGs can be problematic. They are a cutting-edge (Peña Pérez Negrón et al., 2021) multimedium, which on the whole typically centres on inclusivity and – perhaps most importantly for translators – globalisation, but notwithstanding personalisation. Generally, as the term is described in the *Encyclopaedia Britannica*, VGs refer to the totality of interactive games made to operate on a specific platform or set of visual display platforms: mobile devices with screens, consoles usually connected to televisions, computers with monitors, and so on (Lowood, 2021). This already presupposes a few ponderous characteristics of VGs.

First, VGs are a medium unlike books or movies, which are more 'independent from' or 'unreliant on' the device on which they are being projected. To put it simply, the viewer or listener's preference aside, a movie or music data carrier, unlike VGs, should be able to be viewed on or read from many different devices – for example a PC, a console, even mobile phones – if they can decode or decompress them, largely owing to being pre-recorded. This also makes them by default identical – in the sense of narrowly understood content – for all audiences each time they are played, regardless of the device. Graphics and some other elements of VGs, on the other hand, are primarily built 'from the ground up' on the machine, which sometimes requires substantial processing power comparable to that of 3D animation tools. Therefore, VGs typically demand minimum requirements to function properly, alongside recommended technical specifications to function 'smoothly'. A player needs to first invest a sum of money in a device (a computer, console, etc.) that is capable of running a compatible game, which in itself depends on certain specificities of components and the operating system. The devices are also usually upgraded each 'generation' to improve their capabilities and the software that can run on them.[12]

---

[12] One could make the case that because of this, getting into gaming can feel like an exclusive, or in many ways, at the very least, a costly experience. An alternative, however, whereby the industry is bottlenecked in order to force greater compatibility, could restrict their 'cutting-edge' competitive innovativeness. This dichotomy could also be explained by claiming that in terms of inclusivity, gaming itself may simply be unable to catch up with its own immense popularity and the culture surrounding it. Nonetheless, there are innovative attempts to provide a compromise solution to this problem, for example in the forms of cloud gaming, hardware emulation, or retro-styled optimisation, including fan-made 'demakes' (downgraded versions) of the most iconic games – but they are yet to see mainstream use. With the dominance of mobile gaming and a saturated market, a case could also be made that high-end technology usability may after all be

Second, the gaming industry is not as uniform as other entertainment industries. In a sense, it is not unusual for multiple mutually incompatible (for the most part) versions of one game to be in circulation (e.g. a game for a mobile device, a PC desktop, a televised console and, although niche today, special arcades). This may mean it is not clear whether they require different localisation solutions, or if the device's technological specificity should be considered during localisation as well – at least some of the practical issues have to do with different resolutions, the requirement of testing the localisation on each device, and whether or not the game should possess a built-in option to change its language.

The Specificity of the Medium

As previously stressed, explaining what gaming is tends towards the complex. Video games can be considered a multicoded, multisemiotic, multichannel multimedium in combination with their various paratexts, such as manuals, legal and technical information – for example, READMEs – documents, websites, merchandising, patches or updates (Bernal-Merino, 2015: 108), extra purchasables, art, and so on. Consequently, '[t]he quantity and variety of the translatable assets generated by each video game may come as a surprise to people who are unacquainted with these products' (Bernal-Merino, 2015: 107). Elsewhere, Bernal-Merino (2020: 299) explains, 'Video games utilise a variety of storytelling techniques from literature, comics and cinema, adding to this polysemiotic opus the pragmatic dimension of semiotic cues through interaction.' Thus, he suggests that much like pen-and-paper role-playing games (RPGs) and – to an extent – paragraph books, they are uniquely capable of both conveying a narration and allowing the player to (co-)construct stories within the boundaries of the developers' creative vision (see GDC, 2018a: 33:33–54:16).

In a 'classic' tutorial-book on programming a specific genre of adventure games, Tyler and Howarth (1983: 4) considered this interactive personalisation a crucial distinction between VGs and other media:

> Unlike a book, where the sequence of events is fixed, an adventure game is different each time it is played because the player chooses what happens at each stage. By giving the computer instruction in response to description which appear on the screen, the player goes on a dangerous journey into an unknown land.

---

generally accessible to the public in the near future, although it is difficult to ascertain as this trend seems to have again slowed down during Covid-19.

Moreover, they materialise what may at times feel abstract about games –
perhaps partially due to their contemporary diversity – by giving insight
(although somewhat dated in comparison to the complex systems of today)
into what games are (or at least were) at their core – talking about 'adventure
programs' as 'interactive databases':

> A database is a computer filing system which stores information and allows it
> to be called up in a variety of different ways, and it can have all kinds of
> serious uses. The player moves through it, altering or 'updating' information
> as [they do] so. (4)

Bernal-Merino (2020: 299) posits a more contemporary testament to arguably the same notion: 'Players act and react to modify situations through
conversing, running, fighting . . . in short, deciding how they want the experience
to continue.'

Customisability

In comparison to other new media, video games as vessels for narration offer
quite a unique set of characteristics resulting from such complexity, but also – or
perhaps chiefly – in terms of their interactivity. As Mangiron and O'Hagan
(2006: 12) observed, 'Video games as a business sector is known as "interactive
publishing", the naming of which highlights the unique feature of this medium.'

In a way that is barely comparable to other media, video games are, in a sense,
systems that enable players to co-generate stories themselves, within the individual narrative framework, utilising the visual, the aural, the verbal and the
non-verbal (cf. Bernal-Merino, 2016). In other words, video game interactivity
is not only the extent to which a game allows the players' stories to differ from
one another, but also the personalisation of player experience, or the ability of
'an observer' to influence the game's narrative as 'the player', to the point
where they can create their own, distinct experiences through interactions.
A good example of this is the 'sandbox' genre – a metaphorical name that
refers to the potential for the user to decide what is used for the game's
storytelling framework, and how it is used – especially in conjunction with
the robust and often demanding player experience customisation systems of
a related type of games, open-world RPGs.

But Bernal-Merino calls attention to yet another aspect – VGs, unlike other
forms of audiovisual entertainment, aim to motivate and challenge players at
their own level and pace. "They do this by various means, for example,
a customisable avatar, an adjustable difficulty level and relative freedom of
movement and interaction within the virtual world.' (Bernal-Merino, 2007: 30–1).
This account from 2007 seems to describe an environment superbly conducive to

media accessibility. Indeed, over a decade later, we can witness the developing prevalence of localisation customisability (for example, the language of audio and of visuals can typically be chosen independently in contemporary VGs). We can also observe the addition of personalisation toggles, settings, audio descriptions and such like – notably standard to multiplayer games such as *Overwatch* (2016) or *Tom Clancy's The Division 2* (2019) – which strive to even the playing field for players with, for example, colour blindness, limited sight and/or hearing and/or movement.

Novelty

Despite seemingly being defined by interactivity, VGs can offer such a diverse range of experiences that even this fundamental aspect can be contested. Gaming can, for instance, push at the boundaries between a linear VG and a non-linear film, like *Gone Home* (2013) and *Black Mirror: Bandersnatch* (2018), or populate gameplay with cutscenes (in-game cinematics), making the experience more like a film in the process (cf. Larsen, 2017: 471).

Alternatively, in some even more avant-garde cases, games can be programmed to attempt to deconstruct where the boundaries of this unique medium are and what ultimately constitutes a game. *EDEN* (2019) from Missing Mountain, for instance, safely demonstrates that games, like all programmes, if designed to, could unexpectedly take control of the player's machine (not unlike malware), thus compromising the player's acting/active power. In the same way, a game may incite the player themselves to willingly renounce the ability to interact, like in *Progress Quest* (2002), which although itself considered a parody, is said to have pioneered the whole oxymoronically named genre of (not necessarily ironic) 'idle games'. Questions like 'what even is a video game?'[13] are still therefore perfectly valid, especially with regard to localisation, where it may sometimes be unclear which elements are meant to be adapted for the target players.

3 Localisation

3.1 Relevance of Medial Specificity for the Processes of Translation

As indicated by Bernal-Merino (2020: 298) – and pivotal to this Element – (g)localisation of video games requires 'much more than text-to-text translation'.

---

[13] Indeed, it is worth mentioning that this Element refers to the medium and localisation of VGs 'as they are', but there are future ground-breaking advancements, such as advanced virtual reality simulations, ad-hoc machine translation for multiplayer/online communication or complete-immersion input devices, to name a few possibilities, that could completely change how these phenomena are viewed – perhaps once more – if they became a standard.

Assuming a similar position, Dietz emphasises the idea that there are 'unique translation challenges which arise from the specific medium of video games' (quoted in O'Hagan, 2009: 214), which, according to Langdell, may require 'developing games with localisation in mind with a practical focus to elicit pitfalls leading to unsuccessful localisation' (quoted in O'Hagan, 2009: 214). Bernal-Merino (2015: 131) discusses this issue in relation to the processes of translation and, importantly, essentially what we deem to be OSL:

> The fact that translators work from spreadsheets, which is almost always the case [or at least was by 2015], with no access to the actual graphics or to the moment in the gameplay where these graphic-embedded words [OSL] can be seen, makes it more difficult to produce the ideal translation. ... Some constraints remain undetected until the localisation process is finalised and rushed for gold copy (the master copy) and international release.

Bernal-Merino also suggests that successful localisation necessitates translation strategies balancing the locale's awareness of cultural differences: 'legal, religious, and political issues ... may influence ... the success of their [the developers' and publishers'] product' (80), thus pointing to the appropriation of content in terms of 'playability'.

This notion of game-world logic seems pivotal to translation in Bernal-Merino's reasoning that 'game interactivity and immersion through the maxim of playability severely affect translators' tasks which results in video game translation falling somewhat outside of the realm of AVT' (97),[14] since the player's reception of the game can be positively or negatively impacted by the quality of the localisation (41; Bernal-Merino, 2020: 300). It is also central to the pragmatic linguistic quality assurance, with 'linguistic bugs' (drawing on the programming terminology for errors) grouped into four levels from unsellable to 'barely visible' (306). He moreover proposes a similarly formalised qualitative formula for the measurement of playability, resting on eight layers of semiosis and the pragmatics 'elicited' by them to guarantee the developer-intended experience (308). And since 'all signs are semantically intertwined', and the semiotic networks across all possible layers need to be maintained to preserve playability (303), one of the parameters is the appropriate localisation of image textures, although mainly in the context of self-censorship: for example, adding 'clothing to naked body textures' (309).

However, while changes made for the purposes of localisation should not hinder the original's utility, functionality and reliability, it is an imperative not exclusive to just gaming: 'Today's video games are essentially a piece of

---

[14] This heavily relates these notions to accessible game development and shared authorship (cf. Bernal-Merino, 2020: 305; see Section 9.4 of this Element).

software and thus game localisation shares many commonalities with software localisation. The need for 'localisation' beyond translation arose due to the shift to an electronic medium in which the text subject to translation is couched' (O'Hagan, 2009: 212). In other words, as expressed by Bernal-Merino (2020: 299): 'As a complex polysemiotic creation, coded into a digital computer, each of the game assets has to be programmed and activated at the correct time and in the correct place.' So, for example, a localised element should be contained in a similar amount of data allocation and disk space on the device's hardware, while performing identically quality-wise. The localised product should not cause the system to fail in capacities beyond formal programming, like comprehensibility, storytelling, interactibility, or in general, disrupt the player's immersion (the suspension of disbelief) or worsen the originally intended gameplay experience or playability (Bernal-Merino, 2015). What it could mean is that a localised product should in theory be virtually substitutable with the original in these terms. However, to what extent this can be applied in practice is often a contested topic.

3.2 Terminological Clarification

Solely focusing on the topic of VGs and software, the content-oriented distinctions between translation, screen translation, multimedial translation and trans-adaptation (e.g. Gambier, 2004) can be contrasted with the more functional or macro-unit-oriented approaches of terms such as audiovisual translation and globalisation, or micro-unit-oriented terms like product localisation and culturalisation. More complex terms, which can function outside of the boundaries of the aforementioned ones, have also been proposed, like glocalisation (cf. e.g. Bernal-Merino, 2020: 311–12; Patel & Lynch, 2013), the model of transcreation (Mangiron & O'Hagan, 2006: 11), adaptation of MIES (Multimedial Interactive Entertainment Software; Bernal-Merino, 2015: 22) – as perhaps a 'tighter, more functional definition' (39), which 'incorporates the key concepts that set video games apart from other forms of entertainment' (37) – or, in relation to preparation of the product as a whole, GILT practices (Globalisation, Internationalisation, Localisation and Translation; O'Hagan, 2016) so as 'to accommodate different languages and cultures, allowing ... the simultaneous release of titles' (Bernal-Merino, 2006: 23).[15] However, we do not suggest that because some of these terms function hypernymically to the others, they somehow make one another obsolete: 'terminology has spread in all directions,

---

[15] This likely refers to the simultaneous shipment [sim-ship] model: 'a localization model consisting of releasing an original game and the localized versions at the same time in different territories' (O'Hagan & Mangiron, 2013: 10)

with new terms being coined, and old terms being appropriated by the industry to convey new realities' (22).

MAPPING OUT OSL FUNCTIONS AND FACETS

4 Procedure and Scope of Analysis

4.1 Material

Our analysis covers two games: *Tom Clancy's The Division 2* (*TCTD2*) and *Shadow Warrior 2* (*SW2*). The motivation behind this choice is that both games are three-dimensional (as opposed to side-scrollers and technologically two-dimensional games), open-world (non-linear), adult-targeted shooter titles. Both titles also have strong RPG elements, crucially being exploration-driven and rich in textual language. All the while, they have also been professionally localised into – among other languages – Polish.[16] In both games, the Polish version consisted of localised subtitles and a localised user interface, but no dubbing – both games played the original English audio.

At the same time, these games differ in terms of the perspective of the player character (third person in *TCTD2* versus first person in *SW2*), game-world setting (Western versus Eastern, using Eurocentric terminology), development team (studios located in Malmö, Sweden versus Warsaw, Poland) and their roles in the industry (AAA (highest-budget) versus indie), among other variables, notably time of release.

Tom Clancy's The Division 2 is a tactical action role-playing game, as a case study presenting different types and facets of OSL. The game revolves around the events following a fictional bioterrorist attack, initially believed to have been aimed at the population of the United States. Not long after the tragic chain of events that it ushered in, the virus of *Variola Chimera Green Poison*, with its estimated case mortality rate of over 80%, led to the necessity of an unprecedented activation of the classified last-resort federal unit, the titular Division. As the crowd-sourced fan-made encyclopaedia states ('Strategic Homeland Division', n.d.), the player assumes the role of one of these elite sleeper-agents

---

[16] Although *SW2* was developed in Poland, game studios can produce in the English language and later localise the product into the languages native to their development team, or produce concurrently in multiple languages under a premise of 'no one original language version'. In an interview with Suellentrop, Iwiński of CD Projekt Red (a Polish studio renowned for hit-gamifying Sapkowski's *The Witcher* books) commented on this topic: '[*The Witcher 3: Wild Hunt* (2015)] was written, in parallel, in Polish and in English.' He also points to another conspicuous local gamedev matter: 'Historically [in Poland], RPGs were rarely localized well. Localization can sound like you just do the translation. No, actually it's like translating a book but at the same time making an audio version with 50 actors taking part in it [and more]. It's cultural adaptation. It's making sure every single thing fits with the character' (Suellentrop 2017).

equipped with bleeding-edge technology, whose task is primarily to restore societal order and ensure governmental continuity at the brink of destruction, with perhaps most tellingly, their insignia resembling a flame-reborn phoenix and the precept bearing a statement '*extremis malis, extrema remedia*'.

The game is a sequel to the first title, the story of which concentrated on the immediate action of the Division agents during the original outbreak in New York City and its outlying areas set vaguely in the early twenty-first century. The second game focuses primarily on quelling the chaos escalating in the eastern part of the United States and the capital terrain, with the player/ playable character's main objective being, aside from protecting and reinstituting civilian settlements, unearthing any suspected political intrigues connected to the source of the virus.

Shadow Warrior 2, on the other hand, is a comedy-driven quasi-sandbox (in this case, partly procedurally generated) first-person shooter, a sequel in the rebooted 1997 series from the creators of the classic *Duke Nukem*. Story-wise, the game continues to follow the unpredictable life of a fearless and sharp-tongued loner-mercenary named Lo Wang. He is once again tasked to risk his life and limb for gold, fighting mystical creatures and magic-wielding mafiosi to, among other things, rescue a dying daughter of the Yakuza leader from the hands of the Zilla Corp zaibatsu and stop the corruption oozing from the unsealed gates of the arcane Shadow Realm. Being part of the remade original series, the game setting was a given. Yet, with it never being specified to be either China nor Japan (Culture.pl, 2016),[17] the fictional location of the game treads the fine line between facetious fiction and real-world Orient-inspired atmosphere (see Section 6.3).

4.2 Preliminary Remarks

This section should be prefaced by the caveat that because of their oft multi-threaded stories, there are different ways games can be considered 'played through', especially for titles that offer many collectibles, achievements, side-quests and after-storyline content, as well as downloadable content (DLC), which may include expansion packs and extra purchasable questlines.[18]

---

[17] This comes from an interview with two members of the development team behind the game conducted for Culture.pl, a state-run source co-financed by the Ministry of Culture and National Heritage of the Republic of Poland: 'Culture.pl is the largest and most comprehensive source of insight into the Polish culture . . . . For over a decade, the portal has been managed by the Adam Mickiewicz Institute' (Culture.pl, n.d.; translated from Polish).

[18] What is crucial in the competitive context of gaming, but also very much here, is that this extends the many ways we could talk about 'playing through', or 'attempting to finish/beat/win at' these

While both games provided a degree of multiplayer playability,[19] neither of the two play-throughs of the respective titles strictly adhered to multiplayer play-styles, considering the unconventional nature of their main goal: methodical exploration. It is worth mentioning, however, that *TCTD2* is an online-only game, even though one may try to play without the help of other players. Therefore, a marginal portion of the *TCTD2* play-through has included multiplayer, much of which was the exploration of the PvP hotspots, the Dark Zone. *Shadow Warrior 2* was played in single-player mode entirely.

4.3 Methodology

4.3.1 Tom Clancy's The Division 2

Our analysis of *TCTD2* relies on a play-through that consisted of the main storyline campaign (a set of role-playing scenarios within the same narrative structure) completed to its fullest ('100 per cent' of its content with thirty-three out of thirty-three missions completed) as well as some side-quests ('51%' of their content with twenty-one out of forty-four missions completed), DLCs not included. As mentioned, it involved the Polish version of *TCTD2*, taking around 60 hours of playing time. This is approximately 240 per cent of the average player time spent on main-quest play-throughs of this game, as estimated based on the data extracted from two separate submission-based websites dedicated to monitoring and documenting such phenomena ('Tom Clancy's the Division 2', n.d.; 'Tom Clancy's the Division', n.d.).[20]

Because the game is set in a realistic modern American city, many locations throughout the fictional Washington, DC have been decorated with advertisements, signposts and billboards of fictitious brands, as well as often narrative-conveying graffiti, scribbles and tags, all in American English. This solution of 'recycling' graphic textures throughout numerous locations of the game's world is not only immersive but has also, presumably, optimised the game technologically (see Section 6.1.2 for further discussion). In contrast to that

---

games. Players can compete against one another in typical-style gameplay, but also in the completionist [obtaining all of the various degrees of items, or all of them possible] play-through, just to name a few. They can even do *glitchless non-assisted runs* which prohibit the use of game bugs [developer oversights leading to unstable system behaviour, which can be exploited to benefit the player], game modifications, developer debugging menus [or 'cheat codes' – special overlays used during development which usually make the game much easier or force the system to behave in a more 'controlled' manner for *debugging* purposes] or other means of 'cheating'.

[19] *TCTD2* offers both PvP [the player vs. other players] as well as PvE [the player vs. the environment, meaning the game itself, including NPC – non-playable character – enemies] and *SW2* offers on-line PvE co-op [co-operation; collaborative play to achieve the common goal].

[20] See Henry's (2019) article for the developers' declared intentions.

optimisation, however, there were also cases of identical messages placed on two or more visibly distinct textures, for example two advertisements, with the same slogan in horizontal and vertical layout. With this in mind, our computing of the number of cases only included the first of such instances.

4.3.2 Shadow Warrior 2

Shadow Warrior 2, on the other hand, is not a series of games known for taking itself seriously – something that is reflected in the shift in function of the OSL presented within it in comparison to *TCTD2*. An overwhelming majority of its OSL can be categorised as either world-building or humorous. In addition, a great portion of OSL is not in English, which could be explained by the conventions of a Western story located in Asia – but nonetheless, every character speaks English, sometimes even marked, like the protagonist himself.

Some levels in the game were randomly generated[21] and missions could be locked out depending on the story progression. This contributes to the game presenting a different experience for every player – and is substantiated on the grounds of the game's plot and setting in an unstable demonic reality. Despite this being a cohesive *ludonarrative* choice (maintaining harmony between the game's script/plot and the design of the interactive gameplay) as well as promoting game replayability, it made it difficult to gather all the unique OSL data, because of the random nature of level generation. However, since the scope of the research was to simulate a single play-through geared towards extreme exploration, this hindrance is acceptable. In that regard, however, it is possible that there are instances of this title's OSL that are yet to be studied.

The material in *SW2* was gathered using the Polish version of the game in close to thirty-five hours – around 210 per cent of the average regular game play-through of 'main story plus extras' category ('Shadow Warrior 2', n.d.) – with the main storyline finished, unlocking the credits. The game progression of the save file used throughout our research was ultimately calculated to be at 87 per cent – including all the non-main-quest content – according to the in-game statistical monitoring of the campaign's completion. Not all side quests were completed, yet they appear to take place in locations already visited during the main questline, which suggests that at the least all the main OSL content should have been covered.

As in the case of *TCTD2*, the play-through of *SW2* was heavily dedicated to slow-paced exploration of the presented game-world and involved careful scanning of the surroundings of the available game location for potentially decipherable visual–verbal elements, as well as manually capturing distinct

---

[21] Culture.pl, 2016.

elements via the game's built-in screenshot function in order to identify and document a maximum number of instances of OSL.[22]

4.3.3 The OSL Data

The data was collected from the Polish versions of the games, with adequately maximised level of detail and resolution of textures, optimised with the available in-game settings (see Section 2.5.2). In the course of the *TCTD2* play-through[23] we identified a total of over 650 unique[24] cases, with most of them naturally observed to have become progressively re-used around the 20 per cent completion mark of the game's main campaign, with new distinct cases found less and less often from that point. This is not unlike the observed OSL reusability in *SW2*. There, however, the game's narrative places the player in different locations, such as a monastery, laboratory, town, forest or municipality. For each of these, different location-specific OSL 'archetypes' were deployed by the developers. To illustrate this, futuristic holograms were exclusive to the Zilla metropolis, whereas scrolls and books were found in the Yakuza mansion. The specific OSL cases have been observed to be 'recycled' within their corresponding locations. This alternation of these differing OSL archetypes throughout the play-through consequently made it difficult to assess when OSLs started to recycle in this game in a manner as organic as in the more homogenous world of *TCTD2*'s fictional Washington, DC. There were well over 400 unique readable OSL cases overall identified in *SW2*, with over 50 appearing in a resolution that was too low to be read. While the number of cases could be expanded, possibly by sourcing OSL directly from the game's code,

---

[22] While 'OSL' stands for 'on-screen language' (an uncountable noun that is pluralised as 'instances of OSL'), our research team uses it internally in a reified form as a countable noun ('an OSL' or 'OSLs'). For ease of exposition, we have used both forms in this Element, in the hope that readers and future researchers in this field can choose which one suits them best.

[23] Here, the portion of the standalone game that was the richest story-wise was analysed, that is, the player versus environment [in contrast to player vs. player] campaign. As established earlier in this section (as well as Sections 2.5.2 and 9.3.1), considering the nature of non-linear RPGs, unlike other audiovisual media driven by narration, such as easily reproducible film screenings, a single play-through is designed to be virtually always unique. Thus, analysing complex VGs to their fullest, if at all possible, would have to greatly depend on one's definition of 'completing' and 'entirety' and – to an extent much like other media – even the product itself, with various other sources of canonical narrative [e.g. paratexts] on top of theoretically limitless amounts of post-story user-generated [e.g. multiplayer] content.

[24] Entities are not considered 'unique' or 'distinct' if they seem to be the exact instance of an entity that has already been screenshot (see Figure 25 for a juxtaposition of two screenshots capturing the same OSL from different perspectives) or if they portray a different instance of the entity that has already been screenshot (see Figures 9, 14, 16 and 20 for examples of the same inscription seen and captured throughout different stages of *TCTD2*, as well as Figure 31 for two different and unique, albeit similar inscriptions, as captured in *SW2*).

the dataset is currently large and diverse enough to offer a representative qualitative account.

It should be mentioned that these numbers also result from how a single instance of OSL is defined – for example, long blocks of text can be considered a single entity based on our criteria. What we mean by a case will oftentimes comprise a number of relatively independent structures whereby the super-ordinate structure captures the element or a number of elements. However, since OSLs are reused throughout the games, in often unique configurations with other inscriptions, it was possible to intuitively discern which cases of OSL were instances independent from one another and disjoinable in the game's system.

Following the identification and analysis of OSL, we wish to posit that a localisation-oriented account of OSL in VGs needs to consider two major facets: a case's degree of prominence (see Section 5) and its function – or more broadly understood characteristics (see Sections 6–8). One more differentiation we propose (see Section 8.1) is motivated by the technical aspect of how OSL is encoded in the game (either *statically* or *dynamically*). Our discussion in Section 9 supports our points and adopts these three angles to illustrate a range of localisation challenges and ultimately inform the translator's decisions.

As part of the data collection process, OSL cases were captured on graphic screenshots in the PNG format. All cases were holistically examined to identify patterns that served as a starting point for categorisation. The resulting typologies are presented in this Element using what we view as the most representative instantiations. This study is the result of a joint analysis as well as exchanges and negotiations of interpretation between the two authors over a period of several months. In all likelihood, the collaborative nature of this project makes our account more comprehensive and minimises the subjectivity of introspect-ive insights. In that vein, another asset of the study design is that we consulted Michał Mazur, an *SW2* developer, about the findings, not only to put them in perspective but to openly test them from a non-academic industry-informed vantage point.

Such an approach is motivated by the naturally 'open' (relative and non-exclusive) nature of the prominence-based and function-based typologies (see Section 9.5). What we mean by this is that the presented types are either relative – one case can be compared and contrasted against another to determine their respective categories on the prominence spectrum – or non-exclusive – one case can be assigned to more than one function type as long as they can be interpreted from such perspectives from the player's point of view or based on the developers' intention.

4.3.4 The Interview

Aside from analysing the localisation of both games, we interviewed one of the creators behind *SW2*, Michał Mazur, to develop the analysis we present in this Element and include an additional critical perspective. The interview was semi-structured, in the sense that the interviewee had received a preparatory brochure with an overview of specific aspects we could discuss. The brochure also defined OSL using examples (primarily from *SW2*). Nevertheless, the interview was held in a minimally constrained form of a live online conversation, which was recorded and archived. This enabled us to transcribe, translate and integrate the interviewee's input throughout the relevant portions of our analysis in this Element. Owing to the informality of this interview, we were able to elicit valuable 'behind-the-scenes' observations, from the perspective of a game developer, as well as honest feedback on our findings and interpretations. The interview was conducted in August 2021.

5 Attention-Allocation Continuum

5.1 Grades of Prominence

To begin with, instances of OSL will naturally vary in terms of prominence. A relevant caveat applicable here will be that – compared to what is the case in film – the prominence status of OSL in games is more difficult to ascertain. This is because while in a film attention allocation is to a large extent guided – for instance through camera angles and shot composition – the more non-linear games are – leaving aside in-game cinematic sequences – the more the player has the choice and agency to explore locations more freely.[25] Crucially for OSL identification and processing, players – as opposed to viewers – can approach a particular object (e.g. by using the controller to move through the 3D environment, change the camera angle on two axes, rotate the camera 360° or zoom in on the object) and keep it in their field of vision as long as necessary to be able to make out an inscription and possibly even ponder over it.

In the rest of this section, we present a working threefold categorisation within a continuum: with OSL that is prototypically, non-prototypically and liminally prominent.

5.2 Prototypically Prominent Visual-Verbal Components

Examples of the first category – prototypically prominent visual-verbal components – are provided in Figures 2 and 3 for *TCTD2* and *SW2* respectively. The rationale behind categorising these instances of OSL as prototypically

---

[25] This might not be true if there is time pressure in the game, either resulting from the plot, mechanically, or from the conventions of multiplayer gameplay.

Figure 2 Prototypically prominent OSL (in *TCTD2*)

Figure 3 Prototypically prominent OSL (in *SW2*)

accessible is that given their text's size, legibility and colour, as well as their placement in locations that the player is expected to or required to visit, they are arguably highly likely to be noticed by a player.

5.3 Non-Prototypically Prominent Visual-Verbal Components

The screenshots in Figure 4 demonstrate multiple cases of OSL that can be categorised as less than prototypically prominent: 'WAKE UP SHEEP', 'USA

Figure 4 Non-prototypically prominent OSL (*TCTD2*)

IS FUKKED' and 'USA' in the upper screenshot, and 'CERA FAILED FUKK THEM!', 'WE ARE FISH OUT OF WATER JUMPING FOR AIR' and 'YOU ARE A GRENADE AGAINST THE GOVERNMENT' in the lower one. Notably, in addition to factors like text size or legibility, the very fact that these instances of OSL co-occur within a single frame can be an important factor behind their cognitive status. Similarly, the likelihood of encountering the stimulus in the presented world of the game and the frequency of such encounters as part of the play-through will plausibly also have an effect.

5.4 Liminally Prominent Visual-Verbal Components

Finally, Figure 5 exemplifies liminal OSL that arguably will not be identified by most players – unless they happen to approach its optional, secluded location and also intentionally invest time and effort into carefully inspecting their surroundings.

Figure 5 Liminally prominent OSL(*TCTD2*)

The OSL takes the form of a notice – 'PAINKILLERS TAKE <u>ONE</u>! – which is handwritten and partly obscured by a shelf. What is more, there are some salient competing stimuli, most significantly the image of the Great Seal of the United States, since this is supposed to be the interior of the US president's airplane. The authorial intention behind such an element could be seen as ludic in nature, since the assumption that the element is expected to be processed by the player contrasts with its designed exclusivity, contributing to the postulated liminality of its ostensiveness and the ambiguity of its translational status (cf. Deckert & Jaszczyk, 2019).

6 Immersion-Enhancing Facets of OSL in Games

6.1 World-Building

The overarching rationale behind in-game OSL is for it to serve as an 'authenticating' world-building or atmosphere-building factor. Such a function can be ascribed to all the occurrences of OSL. Remarkably, at the same time – as we show further on – OSL can be designed in such a way as to perform other functions alongside the more rudimentary one.

6.1.1 Amount of Language per Case

The screenshot in Figure 6 neatly illustrates OSL's world-building function. At the same time, the image exemplifies the remarkable meticulousness with which these elements are designed visually (e.g. in terms of colour choices and typography) as well as linguistically (in terms of wording), and subject-wise. The player is able to read the text of the parking information shown in Figure 6, including details such as the parking fee for a particular duration of stay as well as some additional details like the note 'Staying longer? Ask inside for our special offers.'

The amount of information provided through OSL can vary from single words to long stretches of text, as shown in the selection of examples in Figure 7. In *TCTD2*, these are: blocks of wall-engraved text relating to American history, then a handwritten whiteboard elaborating on some ballistics technology, followed by a placard with zoological information. All of these are perfectly readable in-game, provided the game's customisable texture quality settings are set 'high' enough (see Section 2.5.2).

Materials showcasing a similar phenomenon in *SW2* were more difficult to capture, however. The inclusion of highly detailed information through OSL may not have been a priority in this game.

If the developers decided that the game's rapid pacing could be threatened by frequent optional linguistic stimuli that encourage longer intervals of processing time, they could have decided against deploying complex OSL structures. In other words, it is possible that time spent on deciphering lengthy OSL text was in this case seen as detrimental to the highly engaging gameplay activities offered by the game, including in-game combat, movement, collectible 'hunting' and plot progression, and was therefore redundant.

Another possibility is that the experience of encountering such stimuli could have been negatively impacted by game optimisation processes. These seem to have included the limiting of the quality of certain graphic components through textural asset compression. A lowering of fidelity (level of illustration clarity and details) may have resulted in decreased readability of more complex texts,

Figure 6 Detailed information in OSL (*TCTD2*)

especially if they were to appear on smaller game-world objects – this seems to be the case with the few captured instances of comparatively more complex OSL cases in this game (see Figure 8). These include: a scattering of various newspapers (in which for the most part only the headlines are readable due to low-resolution textures), container type details (mostly comprising irrelevant numbers) and two low-resolution renderings rich in non-English OSL. One of these is a street-adjacent recycling dumpster and the other an ancient, magical scroll. Another instance of heavily compressed OSL happens to be an homage to a classic Japanese cultural item, shown in Figure 17, discussed in the context of culture-bound and multilingual OSL components in *SW2* (see Section 6.3).

6.1.2 Recurring Cases

A significant mechanism employed to reinforce the world-building function is to deploy variants of a given instance of OSL in a recurring fashion – for

Figure 7 Differing amounts of information per single OSL (*TCTD2*)

example the same brand name, or a slogan with repeated wording – sometimes even likely produced by the same person across locations that can be inferred from handwriting. An illustration from *TCTD2* is provided in Figure 9 with the inscription 'VIRUS IS A PUNISHMENT' alongside two tags; Figure 10 shows a similar mechanism in *SW2*.

As previously mentioned, however, it is essential to remember that reusing assets is useful from a technical standpoint as well, saving storage space on both the original carrier and gaming machine's disk, decreasing the time necessary to download or install the game as well as optimising asset loading and rendering times (see Section 2.5.2). Therefore, this could be another logical explanation for employing such a strategy, besides building the atmosphere of the world presented.

Figure 8 Differing amounts of information per single OSL (*SW2*)

Similarly, it could be argued, however, that due to advances in technology, nowadays there is little incentive to graphically compress textures to the point where OSL is hardly decipherable, unless the developers specifically need just that, or want to improve the accessibility of their game for the users of lower-spec or legacy systems (as well as mobile devices, potentially), which would still be in circulation at the time of release.

On the other hand, retaining low-resolution textures could be seen as maintaining a gaming convention, which stems from the era of game development when authors had to compromise between keeping games' visual appeal and their playability on bygone consoles and computers with limited processing power. Arguably, high-fidelity textures nowadays can add to the immersion and realism of the game's setting.

6.1.3 Realism

One way of adding realism is via wall-inscribed OSL, which is exemplified in *TCTD2*. To increase their plausibility, the game's authors might decide to insert a spelling error, as can be seen in the word 'ABONDED' (Figure 11) – most likely a misspelled variant of 'ABANDONED'.

Figure 9 Textures recurring across locations (*TCTD2*)

6.2 Narratives in OSL

Another discernible function of OSL is to construct narratives, as is notably the case in *TCTD2*. From the perspective of the game's story, the world-building instances fall into two broad categories: pre-apocalypse and mid-/post-apocalypse ones. The former include names of places like shops and restaurants, advertising text and standard information found in streets and on buildings – for example, phone-use restrictions or safety notices. The latter are primarily sprayed inscriptions on building walls, but also realistically repurposed traffic signs (see bottom left in Figure 2), which point to a central property of OSL. Conforming with the notion of environmental storytelling (Fernandez-Vara, 2011), these instances play an important role in building the game's discourse by linguistically representing the society formerly living in the now desolate surroundings.

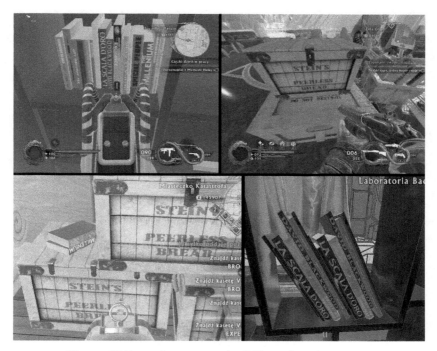

Figure 10 Recurring textures in different locations (*SW2*)

The believability of *TCTD2*'s game-world is reinforced by the plentiful graffiti and street art, as well as cryptic and enigmatic tags, the meaning of which is likely understood only by the game-world artists and, potentially, the game developers. In the process of examining the collected screenshot material, the number of individual inscriptions has been documented to exceed at least 250 distinct, untranslated messages – not including other types of untranslated OSL. A preview list of the verbalised entries can be found in the Appendix. Again, it is worth mentioning that most of them can be observed repeating throughout the game-world, likely to make their discovery more probable – a standard practice for some open-world games – or to enhance realism, as previously stated.

The linguistic evidence of this type, produced presumably by former inhabitants of the city, creates at least two discernible and internally consistent narratives that can be tracked by players. One focuses on the citizens' dissatisfaction with the handling of the crisis by the authorities who, despite potent reaction, ultimately could not prevent the overwhelming chain of events and large-scale destruction. The other provides insight into the routines and struggles of the District's many fractured communities, trying to self-govern during or shortly after the crisis. Both of these narratives are exemplified in the 'stories' represented by the OSL instances in Figure 12.

Figure 11 The 'ABONDED' case (*TCTD2*)

The players can find the OSL presented in the top right-hand corner of Figure 12 by stumbling across a residential district near the Potomac River. The peace and quiet of nature overtaking the garden of the residence coupled with the gigantic banners hanging from its balcony tell an ominous story. The words read: 'NO TOMORROW: END OF THE WORLD PARTY; INFECTED WELCOME – 9 PM' and 'WE WERE BETRAYED'. Those two simple utterances can be interpreted rather unambiguously as a defeatist call for the infected *as well as* those yet uninfected by an extremely contagious, untreatable and deadly disease, central to the game's story, to gather under one roof. What is left, among the stillness of a once roaring city, is a remnant of a desperate carousal for those who have lost all faith in the authorities to save the people in need. What might be inferred here is a story of people deciding to share their final moments in a ghastly bacchanalia, rather than scrambling to survive the end times self-isolating and quarantining. The OSL may thus constitute a piece of environmental storytelling about a slow and horrific doomsday mass suicide – a tale told with just twelve words displayed in a neglected garden.

The second instance of OSL, visible in the bottom screenshot in Figure 12, is expected to be seen by the player during one of the missions, in a staircase of a raider-occupied high-rise block adjacent to a mall, transformed into various

Figure 12 Storytelling function of OSL (*TCTD2*)

drug-making facilities.[26] To interpret this particular instance of OSL, we should briefly discuss the presumed diegetic author of this writing: the aforementioned raiders. The luminescent light-green paint, like the one in which the OSL is

---

[26] Nicknaming them 'kitchens' and 'kindergartens'.

diegetically written, is to be interpreted in-game exclusively as a sign of 'the Hyenas'. The animalistic name of this pack of raiders is likely an intentional device to help the players characterise them among other enemies. The name may relate to their willingness to scavenge and kill with no respect or empathy and is consistent with the conceptualisation of the Hyenas as a savage, dehumanised mass, or an unsympathetic barbaric force opposing the civilisation supposedly represented by the player, who is tasked with bringing them to justice for their crimes against the struggling civilian population.

The OSL in Figure 12 is a green-sprayed imperative to 'TAKE CARE OF THIS' with an arrow pointing to a makeshift barricade. The barricade is presumably a remnant of the early stages of the viral outbreak – a result of quarantining – and might have already been there when the Hyenas settled in. From one point of view, the OSL serves an instructive function (see Section 8.2 for further discussion) – telling the players that the fiends are not to be found upstairs, as they could not have got there without moving the barricade first. The player is thus provided with a believable motivation to instead decide to move downstairs (where their linear mission is heading), rather than upstairs (where they could have gone otherwise, missing their objective).

From another perspective, however, it can also be telling a rather flippant, ironic tale: that the Hyenas' procrastination in cleaning their base has ultimately proven to be the bane of them. Since the barricade can still be seen in their base when it is being neutralised by the authorities (i.e. the player – the Division), the criminals, through their sloth or incompetence, appear to have helped the Division find their way inside. In this sense, the game presents the player with an opportunity to evaluate the Hyenas as a collective. The situation would suggest that their cruelty may be a façade of a fundamentally puny and inept gang – not a truly *organised* group. Using OSL and environmental storytelling, the game invites the player to draw this conclusion themselves.

The previously discussed examples of OSL represent stories that have presumably taken place in vastly different periods of the game's timeline: one before the nadir of the catastrophe and one afterwards. This creates a clear continuity of time in the presented world, which reinforces both its verisimilitude and potentially, the player's motivation to explore. A case in which the two narrational time periods apparently interweave is provided at the bottom of Figure 13, captured in a Hyenas hideout. What can be assumed to formerly have been a market stand selling food – indicated by the signboard 'WAFFLES, SANDWICHES, SOUPS, DRINKS, ICE CREAM AND MORE' – is now probably repurposed to warehouse stolen supplies for the Hyenas – as indicated by the liminally perceptible 'COLLECTION POINT' OSL sprayed on top of it.

Figure 13 The 'WAFFLE BOOTH/COLLECT POINT' case (*TCTD2*)

Incidentally, there is yet another instance of OSL in the same screenshot: the word 'ENTRANCE' is visible deeper into the booth structure. One might be inclined to judge it to be non-prototypically ostensive, yet the small, diamond-shaped marker on the door suggests that the player is in fact expected to go through it to progress through the mission.[27] They are subsequently very likely to read the OSL, thus fundamentally making it a case of the prototypically ostensive structure, by our definition.

6.2.1 Multiple Interpretations of OSL

Another interesting choice on the part of game creators is to include OSL that can have several possible interpretations. In the case of 'KILLING TIME' in Figure 14, there are at least three available interpretations. First, the writing on the wall can indicate the time when killing happened/happens. Second, it can be understood as a gerund variant of the metaphorical expression 'to kill time'. Finally, it can be taken to function as an intertextual reference since there exist at least two VGs, a film and a TV series entitled 'Killing Time'.

The 'Killing Time' case is a neat illustration of variable degrees of asymmetry involved in translation whereby it might not be possible to render the phrase in such a way as to open analogous paths of interpretation. Depending on the structure of languages involved and the expected overlap in the players' background assumptions, some of the layers can be much easier to translate than others. For instance, Polish uses a metaphorical expression of 'killing time' in

---

[27] This displays a certain limitation, bypassed through detailed discussion, of showcasing interactive 3D video game environment and illustrating it with non-dynamic 2D screenshots.

Figure 14 The 'KILLING TIME' case (*TCTD2*)

a fashion similar to English but once this target variant is selected, the other two interpretations may not be available for the TL receptors.

Indeed, some OSL instances could even be seen as poetic due to formal characteristics that prompt multiple interpretations, requiring all the intricacies of a more literary translation approach to successfully localise them. As an example, some claim that 'lineation is the defining characteristic of poetry' (Hazelton, 2014), and indeed, in lyric poetry especially, the intentional insertion of linebreaks can be, among other functions, used precisely to create meaningful ambiguity expressed through that visuospatial presentation (cf. Koops van 't Jagt et al., 2014).

Thus, whether intentional on the designers' part or not, the enjambment of the three lines of text in Figure 15, despite the laconicity, invites comparisons to poetry, because of the dual meaning. The text can either be interpreted as one of the many comments disapproving the fall of Washington, DC to such a ruinous state – as in the exclamation 'Freakin' chaos[!]'. Alternately, it could be seen as

Figure 15 The 'FREAK|IN|CHAOS' case (*TCTD2*)

the alias of the diegetic tagger (the person assumed to have written the inscription) – as in a 'Freak in chaos' – in which case it invites further potential for interpretation. The diegetic tagger could have chosen such an alias precisely because of the play on words – making it more storytelling in nature – or to note their capacity to indulge in their passion of tagging more freely, owing to the authorities being much less inclined to seek out any alleged vandals due to the anarchic unfolding of the game's cataclysmic plot.

In this vein, another example from *TCTD2* is the name 'SLANTER' (see Figure 16). While dictionaries record the word 'slanter' as obsolete, it is also markedly negative, associated with deception. That this name should be given by the game creators to a construction company could be surprising, or perhaps humorous (see Section 7.1 for further discussion) if read as intentionally ironic, especially given the company's advertising line – 'In cooperation with the local community in creating a liveable cityscape' – contrasting with the demolished ruins of the cityscape, housing gangs of dangerous scavengers and fiends.

6.3 Culture and OSL

One of the mechanisms reinforcing the storytelling as well as world-building functions is to embed culture-bound elements within OSL. It is of particular utility for settings that try to convey a sense of realism or are directly linked to a factual location and time, such as the one in *TCTD2* (see Vitka, 2019). This may be why *SW2*, located, on the contrary, in the fictional country Onishima, with its comedic tone, does not seem to offer many examples of English OSL

Figure 16 The 'SLANTER' case (*TCTD2*)

that strengthen its verisimilitude, instead opting for clear authorial *aesthetic* inspirations from various Asian cultures and their art.

Onishima is flauntingly fictional, with mythical demons, futuristic robots and super-(anti-)heroes co-existing there. It presents both rural and metropolitan characteristics of contemporary Japan and China, richly incorporating tropes from classic action cinema, Asian mythology, history, folklore and pop culture of the Far East.[28] In an interview with Culture.pl (2016), Tadeusz Zieliński, then PR and marketing manager for the game's dev team,[29] reveals the following: 'The setting [of the game] was given, because *SW2* is a remake and we needed to keep that part of the original. . . . [T]he entire graphic art was inspired directly by Japan, especially the architecture of Kyoto.' In the same interview, Paweł Kowalewski, the lead gameplay designer behind the game, explains:

> When creating the game we drew on Japanese and Chinese culture in various ways to add flavour to this setting. For instance the characters reference such mythological beings as Gozu, Mezu, Xing, these are Chinese, or Ameonna, the Japanese goddess of rain. . . . There's also Orochi, a mythical eight-headed Japanese dragon. . . . Anime was a big influence, as well as the language.
>
> (Culture.pl, 2016)

It is possible then to consider the non-English OSL of *Oribe Yasubei Taketsune* (1847) by ukiyo-e master Utagawa Kuniyoshi (Figure 17) as not just an easter egg,[30] but on a meta-level (not directly relating to the content of the OSL but its significance as a reference) a device that can operate as both

---

[28] At times even ridiculing some negative stereotypes associated with martial arts, samurais, ninjas, the Yakuza, etc.

[29] Game development team: a holistic term for all creators responsible for developing a given program.

[30] An easter egg is a kind of message – typically a fourth-wall-breaking reference – 'hidden' in a video game by its creator(s).

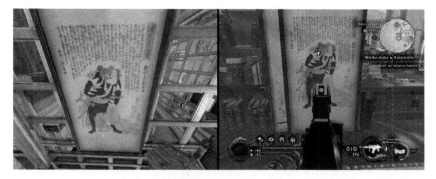

Figure 17 Culture-bound OSL (*SW2*)

a Far East atmosphere-building component and a storytelling piece. It could be suggesting that Onishima is located in a 'post-apocalyptic' Japan – as is presumed by the Culture.pl (2016) interviewer – or at the least that the members of the Yakuza were able to smuggle counterfeit copies of the treasured Japanese piece into its borders, as substantiated diegetically by the reappearance of this texture throughout different locations.

Similarly, the examples from *TCTD2* in Figure 18 portray elements from the American cultural context, while embedding text created by the developers. Their significance arises from being coupled with images of historical figures and referencing an event, such as, in this case, the Second Indochina War of 1955–75.

An intriguing consequence of deploying such an element in localised media is that they will almost certainly not be equally recognisable for players from American, Japanese or other cultural backgrounds. In literary translation, an attempt to mitigate such asymmetry could be made, at least in some part, through the use of non-diegetic footnotes. This even happens, to a much lesser extent, in audiovisual media – as seen in amateur fansubs, where there exists a phenomenon of adding translator footnotes to subtitles (cf. Liew & Che Omar, 2018: 116).

Culture-bound OSL can also relate to other aspects of meaning-making connected to a specific language as well as the socio-culture utilising it. The penultimate culture-bound instance of OSL in Figure 18 has the name of one of the most important political figures in the United States, the Speaker of the House of Representatives, written on stacks of money. This could be read as a critique of the supposed corruption inside the fictional Congress, a version of the 'money = power' metaphor or a general reference to the idiom 'money talks'. Narratively, however, it is implied that this was written by members of a vile gang of scavengers, whom the player is not encouraged to sympathise with.

In the concluding instance in Figure 18, names of historical figures are explicitly inscribed on the wall. While the name Abraham Lincoln will be, at

Figure 18 Culture-bound elements alongside OSL (*TCTD2*)

least on a basic level, familiar to players, irrespective of their cultural background, the name Royal Cortissoz will be challenging even to some of the SL
players, and even more so to those from other cultures.

Figure 19 The 'MONUMENT' case (*TCTD2*)

A case that requires even more advanced background knowledge is presented in the image in Figure 19, an instance of OSL that reads 'LIVING IN THE SHADOW OF THE MONUMENT'. Given the definite article and the location where the game takes place, this is a rather unambiguous reference to the Washington Monument. This interpretation is then corroborated as the obelisk actually emerges in the background. On the one hand, a literal reading of the inscription can be activated – that of actually living close enough to the monument for it to cast a shadow on the building (and the fact that this is a residential building is supported by the laundry drying on a line). On the other hand, a metaphoric interpretation can be activated, with vast meaning-making potential. The coupling of the literal and metaphoric dimensions creates an interesting mechanism for meaning to be constructed but the prerequisite is that players have access to particular cultural assumptions. In reality, these background assumptions will not be symmetrically accessible to players – within cultural and linguistic communities and all the more so across languages and cultures.

Figure 20 presents another case of OSL the interpretation of which presupposes certain cultural assumptions. This instance is additionally interesting because it creatively distorts the name of the US presidential aircraft. First of all, 'one' is distorted into 'gone'. Second, on close inspection we notice that 'O' in 'FORCE' has been reworked for the word to be read as 'FARCE'. If we analyse it even further, the letter 'A' can be decoded as the so-called 'circle-A', recognised as an anarchic symbol.

This case constitutes a localisation challenge on multiple levels. The first possible decision-making crisis point (cf. Pedersen, 2007; Lörscher, 1991) is

Figure 20 The 'AIR FARCE GONE' case (*TCTD2*)

whether to attempt translation in the first place. If such an attempt is made, a major challenge would be to render the layers of signification added through the manipulation of letters in the English name, especially since the plane's name is typically used in its original form when referred to in Polish.

7 Multiple Levels of Communication in OSL

7.1 A Humorous Dimension

The writer's creative engagement with the addressee can assume humorous or ironic characteristics. The *SW2* development team was so prodigious in utilising OSL to contribute to this aspect, that humour in this case could be argued to have become characteristic of the narrative, the game-world's comedic setting and its atmosphere in general. It is possible to say, then, that humorous function in these cases interlocks with the world-building function, which corroborates the claim that OSL functions can overlap.

7.1.1 Allusions

A substantial amount of the OSL design in *SW2* was based on pop culture references, such as the selected few shown in Figure 21, where one of the companies advertises itself with a slogan paraphrasing the lyrics of a popular 1985 rock song by Dire Straits: 'Money for nothing and commission for free'. There is one more notable musical reference, visible in Figure 21. Among alcohol bottles, many of them carrying OSL jokes as well, there is one labelled 'Ace of Spades: Lemmy's spirit', this time most likely referring to the song 'The Ace of Spades' originally sung by Ian Fraser Kilmister of Motörhead – stage name Lemmy.

Figure 21 Pop-culture-bound elements in OSL (*SW2*)

We showed these examples to Michał Mazur, a representative of the *SW2* development team. He elaborated on them, intriguingly implying that indie studios are almost expected to implement tongue-in-cheek meta-jokes. We can speculate that this is to say players appreciate the inclusion of optional fan-serving elements (which could be cut based on time or budget), and is an indication of a passion[31] driving the creative process that is not motivated by profit:

---

[31] This certainly is not to suggest that 'passion' – especially artistic passion, not just relating to the joy from making games – is exclusive to indie studios (cf. Massive Entertainment, 2017), but rather that these elements may simply constitute tangible examples of this for the players. Especially so if they are numerous in the game – thus, although not adding much to the game

> Sure; some people on our team like rock and metal. Perhaps someone
> suggested those [textures] to be included, without telling the higher-ups
> that it's a musical reference – thinking it's so obvious. And the supervisor
> hasn't recognised it. Honestly, I haven't either, at first. Or maybe they've
> just missed it. Those don't get much attention, relative to the bigger
> picture. Another thing is that we are seen as this indie studio – we were,
> now we're no longer 'indie' – so adding these kinds of flavours suits our
> image.

He moreover pointed out:

> I think such initiatives [to add real-life references] might be viewed differ-
> ently in bigger studios,[32] where they risk interfering with the plans, or could
> go against some qualitative rigour. There might even in general be different
> expectations at work. . . . But it does take discipline to, say, leave your work in
> a state that would allow someone else, on another continent, to immediately
> continue it. There must be more transparency [e.g. in the game's code] than in
> smaller studios – these tend to almost be like communes.

From the point of view of translation, such cases are especially thought-
provoking because elements like song lyrics and song titles – as opposed to
film titles – typically remain officially untranslated and therefore are more
recognisable in their original form. Notably, however, the player's ability to
associate an on-screen expression with a particular artist or song does not
entail that the player understands the expression. This gets even more compli-
cated when the SL wording is somehow manipulated – as in the Dire Straits
example earlier on where the fragment 'and your chicks for free' is replaced –
because at that point the semantic content of the expression acquires additional significance, and the player might merely link the OSL to the Dire
Straits song – or even more generally see it as an underspecified musical
reference – without realising that there is more to it in this particular instance.
With this in mind, translation would be a way of offering players a fuller
experience. At the same time the TL should be implemented in such a way as
to enable the player to identify the original phrasing in the first place, as that
would serve as an access point.

Another instance of OSL, shown in Figure 21, can be found hidden on the
textures of a repurposed-tool weapon, a chainsaw. In addition to possibly honour-
ing the legacy of the most esteemed first-person perspective games, such as *Doom*
(1993), which also featured a chainsaw in its arsenal, it carries an OSL – 'FRONT

---

on their own, they might become meaningful globally, reinforcing the playfulness and potentially influencing the player's reception of the game as a whole.

[32] The interviewee highlighted throughout that the practices familiar and intuitive to him may in
fact only be typical of smaller studios with which he has had experience.

TOWARD ENEMY'[33] – on the front side of the weapon. Since *SW2* does not offer any diegetic way to look at weapons from the front-side (being a first-person shooter), without modifications to the game, the players can only find the OSL by looking inside the game's codex for more information on the weapon, making it even more liminally ostensive as an OSL. On top of that, it should be noted that the weapon is named 'Warrrsaw!', an homage to the capital of Poland, where the game was developed (Culture.pl, 2016).

Figure 21 shows yet another noteworthy instance of humorous OSL – 'And all the cake is gone. You don't even care, do you?' – which can be found inside an openable fridge. It is a direct quote from one of the games in the *Portal* series (2007–11), used by an antagonistic artificial intelligence to gaslight the player after they disobey her tyrannic programme. The series even spawned an idiomatic expression, 'the cake is a lie', used throughout media and discourse to refer to a situation in which a person who naively expects a positive outcome is being deceived.

If the intertextual reference to the *Portal* series were to be translated, it would require the translator to consult the target-text variant from that series to enable players familiar with that particular variant to detect the link. Translating the expression from scratch – which would likely be less time-consuming – would encompass the risk of proposing a variant that is simply very different from the official translation, however straightforward and unambiguous the English SL text may seem.

We asked Mazur about the instance of OSL that jokingly references the name of a popular car manufacturer (see the bottom of Figure 21). He revealed a rather unique, innovative perspective to jokes like this, once again relating it much more to the practical dimension of decision-making processes in game development:

> This [solution] is quite established, just like the fictional Acme [the corporation – a running gag in cartoons]. I believe some cars in other games – games by different studios – have also had their logos altered in this fashion. ... We can creatively base our in-game models on the design of branded products, but we can't use their actual names. So, even if we wanted to use a non-fictional name on the textures of that in-game pickup truck, we'd have to ask for permission – probably buy it. But most people should know what [car brand] we've referenced and – since we're primarily aiming for the anglophone market – most should probably get the joke, too.

---

[33] The comedic element is possibly that chainsaws do not require such instructions, unlike, for example, military anti-personnel Claymore mines, on which a similar message is marked for soldiers, as can be seen in films like *Nobody* (2021) or VGs like *Tom Clancy's Rainbow Six* (2015).

Figure 22 OSL engaging the player/the player's persona (*TCTD2*)

7.2 Breaking the 'Fourth Wall'

The quality of provoking thought and inciting the player to utilise the active/ acting role in VG narration can take different forms in games, also with the help of OSL. In Figure 22, we can see curious examples of provocative OSL in *TCTD2* – the graffiti 'IF YOU CAN READ THIS YOU ARE DEAD' and a hacked bygone-era programmable road sign. This once again (see Section 6.2) uniquely merges the two narrative periods – 'pre-apocalypse' and 'post-apocalypse' – and adds to the game's realism, as the programmable sign now displays a vulgar affront: 'FUCK OFF AND DIE', presumably an act of the diegetic vandals.

These two OSL cases creatively draw on the mechanism of addressing their reader, in a process arguably more engaging than that of the more frequent, cosmetic world-building. In a medium where the player is immersed in the role of a character, this creates a direct – and in this case unsettling – relation between the message and its recipient.

While in most OSLs covered in this Element and throughout the game the addressees are possibly both the playable character and at another level the player who controls that character, there can also be less canonical configurations. An example of this, presented in Figure 23, is the abandoned protester sign, reading 'ANGRY SIGN'. The text can operate on at least three communicative levels: firstly, it can be read as a hidden joke among the game developers (see Section 7.3.1); secondly, an easter egg made for the players, intended to draw them out of the player's character role momentarily to appreciate the nonsense of such an odd-one-out; or thirdly, as a story-piece: that of a rallying crowd, with one protester creatively producing a 'meta-sign', which could genuinely be a way of venting anger or possibly even mocking other protesters.

It is also a good illustration of the interaction of sub-optimal OSL prominence and its function, as well as its potential to affect the player. It could be postulated

Figure 23 The 'ANGRY SIGN' case (*TCTD2*)

that the text here is particularly potent, because a number of conditions need to be met for the player to come across it. Firstly, the player needs to stumble across the correct location on the map and not be distracted – for example, by combat. Then, they likely need to intentionally scan for elements to interact with (i.e. OSLs). The sign is moreover located on the ground level, where players might not typically allocate their attention without good reason. Additionally, this 'anomalous' sign needs to be detected among the 'regular' ones.

7.3 Authorial (Quasi-)Intrusion

In that vein, an intriguing case of what could arguably be viewed as language is presented in Figure 24. The game's place of origin is referenced as the binary code reads 'Greetings from Warsaw', providing the players with a riddle of sorts to solve (see Section 8.2), as long as they are able to find the OSL – or consult external sources in order to do so. It adds an infrequent puzzle-logical component if found through exploration in an otherwise action-driven title, and potentially even creates an opportunity for intercultural dialogue.

We asked Mazur if he found this element to be potentially inaccessible to some players, to which he responded:

> I don't think it's anything complicated. I find players to be nerdy enough to read it, or at least recognise what this is and know how to go about decrypting

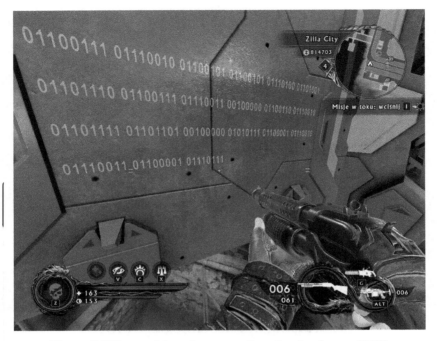

Figure 24 Binary-ciphered message from the developers (*SW2*)

it. As long as they are persistent. I personally wouldn't be persistent enough to write those zeroes and ones down [e.g. into a binary-to-text converter]. (Laughs). But someone surely did. I don't find it that esoteric.

A different, however similarly intricate, case of non-canonical communicative set-up is illustrated in Figure 25. Here the playable character is – at least to some extent – excluded from the communicative event. The participant status of the playable character is inferior to that of the player since it is only the latter who can retrieve the additional layer of meaning communicated by the game's creators. The screenshots illustrate this with a library poster that features quotes from well-known authors. Beside quotes from Oscar Wilde and George Orwell – which are not extremely out of the ordinary for a game set in a realistic world – there is one from Tom Clancy, whose name is instrumental in the game (series).[34] While the playable character can be seen as a legitimate addressee of the quote by Tom Clancy, that character is not aware of being a part

---

[34] It should be pointed out that the development team behind the series, Red Storm Entertainment, was co-founded by Tom Clancy, who said upon its inception in 1996: 'This is a whole new world for storytellers . . . a way for readers to do the telling. Our goal is to define the state of the art in computer games and take it further on from there' ('In the Studio' 1997).

Figure 25 The 'QUOTE FROM TOM CLANCY' case (*TCTD2*)

of a game closely associated with that name and cannot retrieve the reference that had been skilfully deployed by the development team.

Mazur also commented on another possible aspect of this element: its relation to other titles from the Ubisoft's *Tom Clancy's* video game series, rather than to the novelist himself (see Section 8.3.1 for further discussion on the promotional

Figure 26 Logos and signatures as OSL, FWH dev team group photo (*SW2*)

function of OSL): 'This could also be a form of promotion. It's like a little wink towards the players, because I assume the games in the series are similar enough to attract the same [demographic of] players.'

7.3.1 Authorial Exclusion of Meaning

Yet another extraordinary communicative set-up is found in *SW2* (Figure 26; 27). The primary participants this time are the game's developers. The player who detects these cases of OSL will most likely identify them as inside jokes but might not be able to appreciate the references in some of them.

The first case (Figure 26) explicitly presents the name of *SW2*'s game studio and its emblem, alongside a photograph of the team. In the other two samples, the autographs of the *SW2* developers can be found on top of desks in what looks like a gamedev (game development) studio, perhaps that of the game authors.[35] Other developers have their autographs furthermore hidden in a secluded cave in the middle of a demonic forest, among other places. Some of the autographs

---

[35] It is not untypical for games to employ this kind of a joke – for example, in the 2008 game *Fallout 3*, among the locations of the 'Capital Wasteland' [which is what the game calls the post-nuclear Washington, DC], there is one dedicated to portraying the game's dev team headquarters. See 'Bethesda Ruins', n.d.

Figure 27 Possible 'inside joke' easter eggs (*SW2*)

are surnames, others are rather what seem to be aliases or diminutives of the developers' names, which in both cases could cause trouble to players unfamiliar with Polish names when deciphering the function of these texts.

Remarkably, there are cases in which this developer–developer communication is so hermetic that it is virtually impossible to understand for any player based on the information provided in the game, coupled with encyclopaedic knowledge. This is true of the examples in Figure 27. It can only be speculated that the Polish word 'żenada' (pragmatically comparable to the contemporary meme-cultural usage of 'cringe' or 'pathetic' labels) may relate to a stereotype of a Polish malcontent, especially contrasting with the edited-in monocle, twirly moustache and top-hat, a conventional attire of the social elite, which may produce further associations.

Similarly, we would argue, 'Beware of Flying Wild Hogs' – one example of the many variations on this reference – could potentially falsely alarm players who confuse the humorous function of this OSL with a tutorial one (see Section 8.2 for further discussion), instructing them to literally be weary of any flying wild hogs. After all, in the unstable and wacky world of *SW2* it may not be such a far-fetched idea to expect, for instance, a boss fight with a demonic boar, especially if one does not recognise the emblem or name of the studio behind the game.

Ultimately, 'LEAVE THE BUNNIES ALONE, YOU SICK BASTARD!!!' could be a direct appeal to the player and their character, as numerous missions take place in forests with harmless bunny[36] NPCs (non-playable characters), which the player *might have* attempted to kill. Conversely, again, it could be another extra-diegetic instance of dev-to-dev communication, whereby one author scrutinises the other for making the bunny entities 'killable' in-game in the first place.

We shared our speculations with Mazur, asking if he could explain the origin of those OSL textures:

> Those are inside jokes, yes. Shortly before the shipping of the game, one of the developers prepared a batch of such jabs at their colleagues from the office. 'Żenada' relates to one of our team members, who would use this word a lot whenever he expressed his dissatisfaction. The sheep was similar. . . . It had something to do with mocking some stereotype. There's no way anyone would understand these. Though this sort of developer-to-developer communication *should not* surface [so that players could see it]. So again, I can't say this was utterly 'planned'. Someone had the time, thought it would be nice, and added an interesting 'zest' for those who find it. A 'zest' which unfortunately doesn't work globally. It's too hermetic and fairly unexplorable.

Perhaps as an explanation for not removing these cases of OSL from the final or subsequently patched releases of the game, he moreover added: 'When I see something I don't understand, I don't dismiss it as foolish. I'm hoping that players do the same.'

7.4 Multilinguality[37]

Remarkably, our findings also illustrate a trend in *SW2* to insert non-English OSL, using the studio's native Polish language (Figure 29), but also what seems to be Japanese, Russian and German (e.g. Figures 28, 29 and 36). The same can also be said about certain OSL elements in *TCTD2*, especially visible in

---

[36] Except one mission where the demonic forces hide inside some of the bunnies and the player is tasked to hunt them down – likely playing on the intertextuality to *Looney Tunes* [Elmer Fudd] and *Monty Python and the Holy Grail* [the killer rabbit].

[37] This term was proposed by Bogucki (2013/2019: 95) to refer to the presence of more than one language in film dialogue as an alternative to 'multilingualism' (cf. Bleichenbacher 2008), which has been rather commonly used to refer to these phenomena but also primarily functions with reference to language use in (groups of) speakers. In turn, Wahl (2008) uses the term 'polyglot' to characterise films that draw on analogous mechanisms.

Figure 28 Multilinguality in OSL (*SW2* upper, *TCTD2* bottom)

the 'Red Dragon' location, which appears to be a destroyed, raider-occupied Chinatown in the Downtown East district of the fictional Washington, DC (see bottom of Figure 28). This removes the players who speak (only) English from their oftentimes privileged position of being able to assess OSL in its original form, as is the case in *TCTD2* and many other games.

We asked Mazur about the different languages used in the game's 2D graphic design and whether or not we might be over-analysing what was supposed to be trivial. His input was as follows:

> I wouldn't say you're overanalysing anything, but you are missing some trivia. . . . When wondering why a bottle of alcoholic beverage has got an English labelling and a carton of milk a Japanese one, you need to remember the developers are trying to deliver you the whole atmosphere. They try to get the players immersed in the virtual world. A game-world, where Lo Wang . . . could buy his milk locally, but maybe imports something more fancy, like wine. Some things are designed this way, though we have more pressing matters to attend to. So certain slips are permissible. . . . We also make use of certain local archetypes. Arms dealing immediately conjures up the idea of Russky Kalashnikovs or RPGs [or Mosin-Nagants, as in Figure 28]. English and Japanese was necessary to embed the world. Polish, conversely, may have been just a coincidence.

7.4.1 Insertion of Polish

The cross-cultural and cross-linguistic idiosyncrasy of the expression 'Château Srato' visible on a wine bottle in Figure 29 is that, for a non-Polish speaker who is not offered translation and makes no attempt at translating it themselves, it looks innocuous enough as a reference to an actual or made-up wine-making estate. The rhyme itself – while perhaps attention-grabbing – is in all likelihood too little to make the player suspicious about the name's legitimacy. However, for a player capable of decoding the Polish fragment of the French-Polish name, the expression will instantly be clear. Wiktionary.org, a service for crowd-source multilingual dictionaries and etymologies, lists the stem 'srak-' for the adjective 'sraki' and adverb 'srak', and defines 'srak' as a 'vulgar, impolite and abstract answer to the question *jak?*' (Eng. 'how?'; trans. KH), so a response that is purposely diminishing and mocking. Considering the rhyming similarity of 'jaki? – sraki' patterned in 'château – srato' it is undoubtedly supposed to be read as a rather simple verbal joke, possibly meant to ridicule the sophistication stereotypically associated with fine wine.

Other liminally ostensive cases of Polish OSL (bottom of Figure 29) are also notable: the player may come across a recurring three-month folding calendar, with the names of the three months neither in English nor Japanese, but in Polish, contemporarily to the game's development process: 'Grudzień', 'Styczeń', 'Luty' (Eng. 'December', 'January' and 'February' of 2015/16). Likely, the texture was simply scanned from one of the calendars available to the game design artists at the office in Warsaw, functioning as a humorous easter egg, mostly directed at those able to recognise what language the names are in.

Figure 29 Polish OSL (*SW2*)

Similarly, in the headquarters of ZNN (almost certainly a reference to CNN), one of the plot's hotspots of the main antagonist, Orochi Zilla, the players may find various clusters of television screens (see bottom of Figure 29). These bring to mind notions of surveillance and privacy, weaving news items with menacing flashes of other familiar snapshots – including OSL textures that could have been previously spotted throughout the game. Together, they may resemble a collage of subliminal messages, motivating the player to confront Orochi Zilla about his nefarious plans. The screens moreover show seemingly banal photographs, likely to captivate the player's imagination as to how hungry the Zilla Corporation is for even the most mundane information, screened to the masses at will. This evokes the image of cyberpunk dystopias with intelligence-hungry corporations and media conglomerates.

However, these more seriously toned thoughts may quickly be dispelled for players able to spot a rather humorous Polish easter-egg in an instance of OSL at the very top of the television screens cluster. Presented like a banner scrolling across the screen as part of a financial news broadcast, this OSL includes updates on 'WIG20' and 'WIG30', market-value-weighted stock indexes of respectively the twenty and thirty largest companies on the Warsaw Stock Exchange. Without acknowledging this immersion-breaking component, the scene will most likely be interpreted as predominantly eery or contemplative, once again creating potential for an almost completely different interpretation of the scene's atmosphere, depending on which optional linguacultural elements are recognisable by the receptors.

When asked if these elements were directed at Polish players or perhaps were to spark interest in the Polish language among people from other cultures, Mazur responded with doubt:

> I don't think so. The wine was designed so that it could realistically have had such a proper name, Srato [and one might not necessarily know it's Polish]. ... We didn't really talk much about the implementation of those assets. No careful calculations of like, their overall 'serious' to 'funny' ratio, or anything like that. Usually, the way we design these is just like you'd think we do. We sit in a room, just the several of us, joking around. ...

Figure 30 presents a comparison between the in-game OSL of a signboard and a photograph[38] portraying a kiosk in Gdańsk (Poland) from 2012. This case of OSL stands out for a few reasons, which at the same time make it a translation challenge. First, the Polish noun 'buch' – in addition to denoting an exclamation referring to a sound caused by an object hitting something suddenly and strongly – can more informally refer to inhaling smoke, which seems to be the intended reading in this particular instance.

Another layer is created by the graphical design of the OSL, its font, colour palette and non-linguistic elements, which allude to the branding of a Polish newsagents' chain. The company's kiosks are commonly found in Polish streets, which makes that visual style fairly easy to recognise. However, the allusion becomes virtually unambiguous when the name of that company is considered – 'Ruch'– which differs in only the first letter from 'Buch', and that word-initial alteration is not major given the visual similarity of 'B' and 'R'.

---

[38] Made available to the Wikimedia.org repository under a Creative Commons licence, courtesy of Artur Andrzej. Logo trademark of Ruch Marketing, Spółka Z OO/Ruch SA.

Figure 30 In-game 'BUCH' OSL (*SW2*) versus real-world RUCH stall

The cultural-embeddedness of the name is clear, with its physical presence in the cityscape, but we can extend this by considering at least one eminent case of 'Ruch' making a film appearance. It was in a cult 1980 comedy *Miś* (*Teddy Bear*) directed by Stanisław Bareja, where a scene takes place at what is in the dialogue referred as 'kiosk Ruchu'. In that scene, one of the sources of humour lies in the fact that the shop's goods include fresh meat that can be bought unofficially, both metaphorically and literally 'from under the counter'. For a receptor with no specific background assumptions – about life in Poland under communism – the scene would be hard to parse, assuming that the receptor got to see the film (or scene), possibly thanks to the OSL in *SW2*, in the first place. Finally, the notion of multilinguality acquires an additional dimension since 'Buch' could be decoded by some players as a German word ('das Buch') for 'a book'.

For a player who cannot decode the Polish expression to then associate it with marijuana smoking, and who cannot access the RUCH/BUCH allusion because of insufficient cultural assumptions, a partial hint comes from the image, as a cannabis leaf is visually represented. Therefore, the central component of the message is cross-culturally secured, but the additional finer layers of meaning will not be accessed across languages and cultures.

Mazur also pointed to an aspect that we have only fleetingly covered in our analysis – the reusing of textures across completely different games:

> But there's another juicy thing. This asset ['BUCH'], if I remember correctly, comes from our older game, *Hard Reset* [from 2011]. Sometimes, the reason a certain asset is added to the game is quite prosaic: if we've got it in our archives, if we've retained the rights to use it and if we need to plug a texture-hole somewhere in the gameworld, we might be tempted to 'recycle' such a texture from earlier. Of course, everything's within the remit of the art director. But assets alternate throughout the games of the same studio, unless their rights of the assets get reserved.

He did, however, agree that the BUCH/RUCH allusion is deliberate and is an example that creates meaningful asymmetry of reception between the locales:

> Certainly, this is an asset that is suitable exclusively for the Polish audience. It is much too exclusionary, as it's been reused from a game made by roughly thirty people. I suppose someone added it [into *SW2*], everyone laughed, and that's just why it stayed. ... That's not the way to go about it, though. [It should be] something more inclusive, or at least something more aesthetically pleasing. (Laughs).

He then elaborated on the decision-making process in terms of the deployment of humorous elements:

> We try to consult everything we do, so as to never cross a certain line. But in the end we are just people. Some things may get 'smuggled' rather incidentally. ... Another thing is that the *Shadow Warrior* series is almost 'notorious' for its earthy jokes. People downright expected that. I personally find [ideas like] Chateau Srato to be a bit on the weak side. But for the record: plenty of our ideas are like that. (Laughs). ... The times are changing though, in a positive way; it's good to be wary.

7.4.2 Foreignised English

In an interview with Culture.pl, Tadeusz Zieliński commented on the cross-cultural aspect of *SW2*, alluding to the fascination among the development team with the land of the rising sun, saying it was intriguing for 'a bunch of Poles basically, to draw on a foreign culture and play with it in a creative way'. Paweł Kowalewski moreover adds: 'Even though Shadow Warrior is set in Asia, it includes plenty of references to American culture' (Culture.pl, 2016).

This could account for the curious usage of English that is stylised to resemble or even repurpose Japanese kana in OSL (Figure 31). This, combined with the characteristics of the fictional Onishima, leaves ample space for story- and atmosphere-related speculation. Better still, since the respective signs can be found in the many districts of the gargantuan (relative to other locations in the game) Zilla City, they have most likely also been implemented with an instructive function in mind (see Section 8.2 for further discussion), to indicate which part of Zilla City the players are visiting.

Furthermore, the English in *SW2* can also be polonised: 'The Metropolis Tajms' (Figure 32), possibly a reference to then newspapers *The Metropolitan* and *The Times*, rendered 'times' phonetically into Polish.

These cases convincingly show that multilinguality in VGs can be put to use in highly creative, if translationally demanding, fashions. At the same time, the

Figure 31 The 'EAST DISTRICT/LEVEL' case (*SW2*)

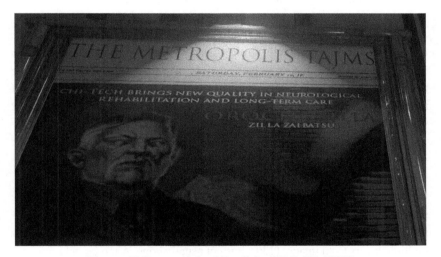

Figure 32 De-anglicised English: 'TAJMS' (*SW2*)

examples show that OSL successfully serves as a vehicle for nuanced uses of multilinguality in multimodal media, which has so far remained under-explored not just in VG localisation but also in film-centred audiovisual translation more generally, where multinguality has been researched quite extensively with a primary focus on language coded aurally (cf. e.g. Badstübner-Kizik, 2019; Bogucki, 2016; Parini, 2015; Chiaro, 2010; for an overview, see Chiaro & De Bonis, 2020).

8 Practical Considerations in OSL Deployment

8.1 Mechanically Discernible Patterns of Other OSL Typologies

At this point, it is necessary to indicate that OSL can also be categorised by way of how it is wired into the multimodal machine of the VG. It seems to be possible for OSL to be coded into the programme in different ways, either 'statically' or 'dynamically'. *Static* OSL is referenced and loaded from a ready-made graphic file, while *dynamic* OSL, although sometimes pre-programmed, can also be 'mechanically' generated in real time. The former can be semi-dynamic in a sense that it could display technically static, but visually dynamic material, such as short video clips or animations. Static-type OSL is also observed to be typically non-interactable. The latter's main function seems to be interactive in order to utilise its changeableness. The *dynamic* type also seems to typically provide non-diegetic information – although this is not always clear, as will be discussed later in the analysis of Figure 33. It is also worth considering that developers, like any creative artists, break conventions depending on their vision – there is no 'one' way to make VGs.

In all the cases studied here so far, 'non-static' (dynamic) instances of OSL appear to be created through string variables (programming code used for storing, displaying and manipulating words or sentences *impromptu*), rather than graphic game textures (two-dimensional illustrations rendered on top of three-dimensional models – 'coating' in-game 'skeletons' of the presented world's architecture, characters or objects – and capable of portraying any graphics, including words or sentences) (cf. Bernal-Merino, 2015: 86). This division seems crucial, because the localisation process typically covers the translation of string variables in textual formats (Bernal-Merino, 2015: 86), as they are easily editable/customisable (see Unity Technologies, n.d.). Perhaps since texture modification is a rather invasive process,[39] which requires graph-ical processing in dedicated editing software (86) able to 'seamlessly apply multiple layers to an image' (130), it is not usually done. A moderately frequent exception to this was the act of (self-)censorship in games, as the law or the market's culture may necessitate graphical changes in order to be able to distribute games officially with no impediment (92). It therefore does not seem to be a coincidence at all that the image/texture variant of OSL is translated much less often in any capacity, even though it is the string/text variant of OSL that appears to be widely under-represented, going by the sample in our study.

We have consulted Mazur on whether a categorisation into textural/static and textual/dynamic elements is sensible for him as a developer and what termin-ology would be most intuitive from a programmer's perspective, upon which he remarked:

---

[39] 'A multilayered graphic file format is needed in order to be able to edit the text neatly without altering the original art style' (Bernal-Merino, 2015: 130).

Figure 33 Dynamic string-based non-textural diegetic OSL, translated into Polish (*SW2* left; *TCTD2* right)

> Earlier on, you used the word 'string', which we use as well. In general, when I add string-texts to the game, they don't say, for example, 'Ammo bag'. Instead, I write down the technical variables which link to a file where all the translated texts are stored, that then get generated in-game. The variable's name goes something like '01InfoCard08b'. Then while we're building a given language version, there's another tool which imports the correct translation of the original text [e.g. 'Ammo bag'] from a reference file and puts it in the place of the link [i.e. the '01InfoCard08b']. That's how the correct text appears in-game in the correct language for the given language version, using a font. The other texts are differently implemented – they are as if inscribed with a crayon on top of the textural graphics.

The example on the left in Figure 33 plays with the idea of a prophecy hidden inside a fortune cookie that can be found in the game-world. The visible text is a string instance of OSL translated into Polish, showing a fake quote, attributed to Shakespeare.[40] Much like in other instalments of the Shadow Warrior series, the player can find fortune cookies scattered around the game-world to fill achievement gauges, but also functionally be rewarded with humorous aphorisms and – fictional or factual – quotes from famous authors, including but not limited to Oscar Wilde, Agatha Christie and Philip K. Dick. Moreover, it is noteworthy that, although the cookies are secrets for the players to seek out through the game levels – thus limiting their prominence in the game-world and the player's access to all OSL instances inside[41] – the quote displayed upon collection is on par with the always-visible non-diegetic player HUD (a heads-up display – an interface, often communicating status information like the played character's health, the game level map, the weapons' ammunition counters, etc.) as it appears on the user interface for a few seconds. As

---

[40] The original English text says 'I figured it out, you guys. It's 'to be'. (Shakespeare)'.
[41] At least with no access to third-party repositories online.

a result, their ostensivity can be categorised as prototypical and this instance of OSL can be comparable to subtitles. This comparison could lead to an argument that their status as an element of the presented world might be liminal – rather than diegetic – but the immersive visuals and the animation simulating the opening of a fortune cookie that plays upon collection suggest the opposite.

The screenshot from *TCTD2* in the right of Figure 33, lastly, showcases an extraordinary instance of an arguably highly diegetic user interface. In *TCTD2*, the played character is equipped with a fictional enhanced-vision augmented-reality technology known as ScanTek, part of the Division's special ISAC field system[42] for all its agents. This, quite inventively, suggests that the player's HUD, in addition to mediating player–played character communication, is an element of the presented world for the played character, as much as any other element seen on-screen. The mechanism here is presented in-game as 'ScanTek's ECHO system', a fictional piece of technology able to spectrally reconstruct the events from certain crime scenes. The technology is used by the Division agents to investigate crimes. When the player interacts with some of the crime-scene-related prompts visible on the screen, the game plays an in-game cinematic of the events that have transpired. The prompts themselves provide brief summaries of those cinematics – like the status of the victims and evidence. They are unfortunately quite cosmetic, as the player has limited agency over the investigation quest-line itself. Despite this, they are translated into Polish and appear to be string OSL.

8.2 Hints, Solutions, Puzzles and Riddles

The first screenshot in Figure 34 presents another example of string-based OSL, with the preview of an upgradeable character-skill item – not untypical for RPGs – which contextually visualises its properties. In this game, the item is stylised as a Magic-The-Gathering-esque collectible card and portrayed as such as an in-game object, possibly in diegesis. Its ostensivity, compared to that of the fortune cookie, is more nuanced, as the contextual prompt appears only when the player comes close enough to interact with it. The preview text itself, however, functions almost non-diegetically, instructing the player of the upgrades their played character will be able to utilise after collecting the item. It has been, perhaps consequently, fully localised, with the use of dynamic textual OSL layered on top of the non-OSL graphic texture of the contextual prompt.

A different example of an instance of OSL that functions tutorially for the player is a piece of cryptic writing on the wall, referencing *The Wizard of Oz*

---

[42] See 'ScanTek', n.d.

Figure 34 Dynamic (uppermost) and static (lowermost) OSL of tutorial function (*SW2*)

(1939), which can be seen in the second part of Figure 34. Seeing that this instance of OSL is placed backstage of a live music space, the player may be led to believe it might not be accidental for the game's authors to use a quotation like that in such a fitting place. They may consequently be tempted to disregard the advice to 'pay no attention to that man behind the curtain' and start to investigate the collision-less (traversable) door further down the corridor. Thus, they will fulfil the actual intention behind the implemented OSL, as they will then be able to find a secret 'developer room' and be rewarded with in-game collectables and easter eggs (some of which can be seen in Figure 27).

We asked Mazur if it would be possible for this OSL to be of a string-type, instead of texture-type and if it would be possible to then translate it, to increase the accessibility to this crucial instruction. Notably here as well, we prefaced this by saying we have not set out to criticise their work, but to look for potential long-term solutions to language-version asymmetries. He answered:

> That's a good idea. It could've been done like that. But I'm not sure. Would it not have made it too obvious, had it been the only element like that to be translated? It would depend on how often the translated language cropped up in situations like these. If we were to consistently do that, then sure. But let me just remind you [about making it too obvious]. Somewhere, there must have been another, more universal indication that a secret is nearby: a dragon pictogram. So this is already a repetition of such an instruction [to seek out the secrets].

As mentioned before, OSL can also aid navigation throughout a complex level geometry. Figure 35 shows a typical example of this from *SW2*. The player's mission is to obtain access to 'Level 3'. The OSL informs them that they are currently on 'Level -2' in the Zilla Lab location. This may already suggest the general direction they ought to be headed: upwards. An instance of OSL almost identical in function can be found in *TCTD2* (bottom-left in the same Figure 35). During one of the missions, a map of a multi-level building is drawn in a prototypically ostensive manner next to one of the doorways. The map contains details explaining the different stages – 'control room', 'metro', 'silo' and so on – which the player will have to fight their way through. Acknowledging this, the player can proactively prepare a suitable tactical plan for the location's raid, for example using a manoeuvrable weapon or melee weapon to reclaim the cramped control room, thus preserving heavy ammunition for more open zones, such as the metro, or the silos.

In the same game, a similar function can be attributed to OSLs found throughout the operational hub for the DC Division agents (bottom-right of Figure 35), the White House. The fictional White House accommodates multiple resources for the players, ranging from useful to pivotal for the game's progression. These include: the clan's base of operations, the bounty officer room, the munition vendor, the equipment re-calibration station, the shooting range, the specialist quartermaster and the rally point (used for cooperation matchmaking – finding others to play online with). The directions to all these locations are correctly indicated by arrows and OSL throughout the White

Figure 35 Tutorial function of OSL: Navigation (*SW2*; *TCTD2*)

House. It might not be far-fetched then to assume that the OSL in the hub is not exclusively for aesthetics and realism. Since players need to frequent the White House, the developers might have suspected that some players could require additional instructions to fluently navigate such a complex base of operations.

While discussing the typologies, Mazur also remarked that this sort of OSL tends to be useful in multiplayer games, where players of the same team can use call-outs to quickly relay important information while locating it on the map using the laconic OSL information, like 'level B'.

8.3 Marketing

8.3.1 Promotion and Recommendation

As suggested by Mazur, both *SW2* and *TCTD2* exhibit another function of OSL, although neither of those titles belongs to the genre of games best known for using it. Racing and sports games often try to simulate the real world to the extent possible, with new instalments from flagship series like EA Sports' *FIFA* (1993–present day) developed annually, in part to promote how far their producers manage to utilise the newest technology to increase realism in comparison to previous iterations. It may not be surprising for players to see actual product placement on digital banners at the edge of the football pitch, or alongside the race-track, near the finishing line. Their use could even be expected, as without such advertisements – with tenuous replacements – the games could feel less like the experience of a real match or a real rally. Such marketing via game textures, if linguistically charged, would match the definition of OSL advanced in this Element, with their function being to uniquely promote a real-world consumer product or build its brand recognition.

Mazur talked about his suspicions about sponsorship in simulation games, linking it back to the aforementioned practice of avoiding the usage of actual names of factual brands (e.g. car manufacturers) in games:

> I assume if you saw something advertised in a sports-game that you wouldn't see during an actual [e.g.] football match, that could break your immersion. So the developers may try to strike up believable sponsorships. And I doubt that it's done for free. Transactions like these are made to suit both parties' books.

This is, however, a delicate subject. Such advertising deployed in the world of a seriously toned non-simulation game has – perhaps peculiarly, given this practice is widespread in other pop-cultural media – in some cases been a source of controversy. In a highly immersive medium such as VGs, the atmosphere of a presented world could perhaps be particularly spoiled for some players when they are intrusively reminded of it being a piece of fiction. A popular recent example is the inclusion of factual brands in the post-apocalyptic game *Death Stranding* (2019).[43] Keith Nallawalla from the advice website Good/Bad Marketing commented on this as follows:

> [a]s most films and TV shows take place in fictional versions of real life, it makes sense for people to be eating, drinking or wearing real products or to see real locations or stores in the background. In video games it feels a lot more forced and can take you out of the experience a little bit, especially if the game has no other real products except for just one thing. What also makes this weird is that older games that have been re-released on newer consoles will often have product placements replaced with generic alternatives. (Nallawalla, 2019)

---

[43] See Campbell, 2019; Lloyd, 2019; Kain, 2019.

Figure 36 Promotional function of OSL (*SW2*). 'Alienware logo' & 'Alien Head Design' ©® Dell, Inc.

8.3.2 Fictional 'Product' Placement

Some games, as mentioned earlier (Figures 21 and 30), opt for generating such 'alternative products' as a means to avoid legal trouble or, less trivially, to enhance the world- and story-building aspects – for example Nuka Cola in the long-lasting *Fallout* series, the addition of which established a tone of satire and humour contrasting the bleak, post-apocalyptic setting.

Shadow Warrior 2 provides ample examples of promotional OSL, too, but many of them do not seem to be product placements *per se* due to two main reasons. First, most are hidden away from the players, like the names of the games *Juju* (2015) (the same studio as *SW2*) and the then upcoming *Ruiner* (2017) (the same publisher as *SW2*) – in secret rooms, as shown at the top of Figure 36. Second, they are incorporated into the world of the game in a way that makes it difficult to discern whether they are fictional or not – for example, the OSLs at the bottom of Figure 36, one using the name Flying Wild Hog almost as if it were a clothing company, the other two referencing a factual brand alongside what seems to be a fictional one (Rodont), but curiously suggesting these are games or arcade stations, which in reality is not the case.

Mazur was also asked about the nature of promotional elements in *SW2*, to which he responded:

> There are in-game arcade machines with visuals of other games, like *Hard Reset*, *Serious Sam* or *Hotline Miami*. I speculate that our publisher initiated those, since they also happen to be their publisher. I suspect it's a marketing strategy, so that those games stay in circulation, get sold in some bundles. This may be a form of brand-building.

Adverts appear in *TCTD2*, too, and their damaged state reflects the diegetic apocalyptic events. Examples range from made-up fast-food chains ('Admiral Burger') and carbonated drink companies ('Lix cola') to fragrance manufacturers ('Merét aroma') and clothing retail companies ('HxC'). While some of them may resemble real-world counterparts, they are arguably functioning as world-building – and to a lesser extent storytelling – components, not as a promotion of real-world existing brands. Since the game world of *TCTD2* is verisimilar, it could however be argued that this type of promotionally functioning OSL would not be out of place in its setting. Yet it could, perhaps, shatter the thin line of illusion of believability for some players during gameplay, especially those who are able to recognise product placement marketing strategies and interpret such procedures negatively – which might be why *TCTD2*'s dev team have not prioritised this function in their game's OSL.

MEANINGFUL MISMATCHES: FINDINGS AND FUTURE DEVELOPMENTS

9 Discussion

9.1 Diversity in OSL

What the discussed cases of diegetic OSL from the Polish versions of *TCTD2* and *SW2* notably have in common is their perceivable tendency to be worded in the source language in both the source and target versions of the analysed games. Static OSLs also appear to remain untranslated more than dynamic instances in the localised Polish versions of the two games. This, we argue, magnifies the mismatches in what meanings are constructed by players across linguistic and cultural boundaries. When it comes to differences, as we have demonstrated, the cases of OSL identified in both *TCTD2* and *SW2* vary qualitatively and functionally. The findings therefore make it necessary to expand the functions proposed by O'Hagan and Mangiron (2013: 162) – drawing on Reiss's (2000) functional typology of text types – beyond 'informative and cosmetic' or cases where such text is 'used for the third-party advertisement of a product', which they alternatively summarise as 'informative/expressive function to give the player certain information such as clues in an authentic atmosphere' (O'Hagan & Mangiron, 2013: 156).

First, OSL is implemented to functionally strengthen immersion, by creating a more believable presented world (with road signs or graffiti), and to contribute to the process of atmosphere-building (e.g. through the utilisation of cultural references in both games). Second, it can be employed as a narrative device, to convey a game's lore (e.g. the civilian stories from before, during and after the incidents of *TCTD2*) or to help understand the overarching plot. Third, it can serve to entertain the player by pulling them from the game-world with a brief, less serious moment of meta-narration (e.g. the many gags of *SW2* or the appearance of Tom Clancy's name in *TCTD2*). It can also serve the purpose of promoting real-life products (e.g. *Juju* and *Ruiner* in *SW2*). This also relates to the capacity of more prominent instances of OSL to grab the attention of the player to instruct them or provide with details that could be useful in-game – especially strategically, as was the case with the numbering of levels in *SW2* and naming of rooms in *TCTD2*. In certain cases, it can even be used to further gameplay, as was the case with the OSL hints of secrets in *SW2*.

This does not mean there is no potential for other sub-categories to be discerned from the general ones proposed; for example, relating to the communicative potential of 'fully' customisable *spraypaint* textures[44] or inter-player conversations,[45] arguably a sub-function of storytelling. There is also the educational value of players learning some history of the United States – as rendered at times in *TCTD2* – or – if they are engaged enough to translate from other languages on their own – exploring the multilinguality of *SW2*. Such an educational dimension can, for example, be seen as a sub-category of the tutorial function.

A dimension to be further explored is OSL optionality and how OSL may influence advancing in VGs. It could be postulated that if an instance of OSL is deployed to assist the player in progressing through the game, the developers should also consider creating early-stage frameworks allowing for the translation of such elements – for example making those particular cases of OSL dynamically typed, for ease of localisation. In fact, there seem to exist cases where OSL identification is 'required' for the player to progress, although a case like that has not been identified in either *SW2* or *TCTD2*. It is worth noting that the understanding of 'being required' and 'to progress' does not seem that

---

[44] In games like *Team Fortress 2* (2007), as well as many other PvP multiplayer games, especially those running on the Source game engine, players can choose up to one custom *spray(painting)* by importing their desired image (in JPG, BMP, etc. formats) from their computers into their game. This allows them to 'spray' this single custom texture on the regular game textures. All players by default are able to see other players' *spray(painting)s*.

[45] As long as the definition of OSL can be applied to in-game chats, as perhaps diegetic communication between the role-playing avatars, rather than the players behind them.

straightforward in the context of gaming. First, it may mean that an instance of OSL simply hints at or relates to – which itself may present a spectrum of options – the progression of the main story, thus *helping* the player come to the required realisation on their own. For some players, that much might be *required* to progress – as is likely the reason an instance of OSL of such a function was implemented in the first place. Second, it may also mean that an instance of OSL functions to enable a deeper understanding or 'fuller' completion of the title – opening further content of the game or the game's series to explore.[46] Third, it could entail the 'expectation' that the player finds the OSL element on their own, processes its content and utilises it to, for instance, solve a puzzle. Such is the nature of many linguistic riddles, exemplified in detail by the localisation of a 2011 video game *Batman: Arkham City* (cf. Bernal-Merino, 2020: 297–312), or many of the puzzles in the atmospheric survival horror/thriller video game *Silent Hill 2* (2001).[47] Alternatively, one could use the example of the Alternate-Reality-Game-esque promotion of the *Portal* series, which required the acquisition of a username and password from an instance of OSL on a wall in the original *Portal* (2007) to be used in a website outside of the game. Lastly, it is worth mentioning that entire game premises can be based on the manipulation of OSL, by proxy necessitating their retrieval to even play the game, such as in the rather unconventional game *Baba Is You* (2019), inspired by computer/programming language.

Mazur suggested that he would categorise OSL elements, broadly speaking, as either essential or optional to the game. The essential ones would be immersion-building, while the optional ones would be fan-serving, in the sense of, for example, easter eggs. The cases of the latter type, he says, are 'inserted at the final developmental stages, because the game could be shipped without them'. This pragmatic view also allows for more liminal cases, like our examples of the tutorial function. As Mazur stated: 'Yet another thing are the elements that help the players move around the world . . . . I suppose those might entail some issues in [language] localisation, though.' Relating it to navigation through the game-world using OSL, he thus also opened up a discussion on the localisation of such elements, pointing to important considerations such as

---

[46] However, with the advent of dedicated game forums, wikis, YouTube channels and other spheres that enable the sharing of information inside fandoms, game progression, strategies and solutions as well as optional easter eggs have been well-documented in comprehensive guides on the Internet, positioning it as the primary resource for invested story-analysers and achievement hunters, as well as gamers who struggle to progress further into the game.

[47] For example, during the clock puzzle of *Silent Hill 2*, depending on the level of difficulty, it can have the player understand the linguistic connection between three names (Henry, Mildred and Scott) visible on an instance of OSL and the three hands of a clock (hour, minute and second). See 'Clock Puzzle', n.d.

space constraints (cf. Mangiron & O'Hagan, 2006: 7) and resources required for such processes. He added:

> I do wonder how people from cultures without the Latin alphabet view that Wang Cave banner [the diegetic, untranslated instance of OSL on top of the Wang Cave location; not the translated name appearing in non-diegetic contexts]. ... Well, theoretically, one could localise those [location names, using the Cyrillic script, hanzi, kana, abajad, etc.] by changing the 3D model. But that is problematic. And again, certain languages might need a lot more space than originally allocated.

9.2 Attentional Resources and Competing Stimuli

In a broader psychological perspective, the cognitive mechanisms discussed in this Element can be accommodated within a line of inquiry into the selective nature of attention, as mentioned in Section 1. Given that the observer can only concentrate on a 'small area of the visual field at a given moment ... in detail' (Zhang & Ling, 2013: 3) and at any given occasion a multitude of stimuli is available, only a subset of these stimuli will effectively be attended to. A notable explanatory notion is that of change blindness, which dates back to the nineteenth-century observations of William James, essentially entailing that detecting changes is possible through attentive focus. This phenomenon has been researched and proven to occur frequently (cf. e.g. Simons & Rensink, 2005), with experiments yielding connected findings (Hall et al., 2010). One of them is especially pivotal for the understanding of the importance of visual stimuli in VGs, and came to be known as inattentional blindness (Rock et al., 1992). It denotes cases where despite one's ability to discern an unexpected stimulus in other situations, they go unnoticed where attentional resources are allocated elsewhere, as convincingly argued based on empirical findings (Chabris & Simons, 2010).

This is eminent for the discussion of attention allocation in a component-stimuli setting because VGs, as audiovisual products, are by their nature heavily reliant on simultaneously presenting the player with elements that can be considered as 'competing' for their selective attention. Thus, many of them can potentially go largely unnoticed by the player-base, pointing to interesting questions, as phrased by Berry (2015: 60):

> Simply along visual lines, computer hardware has rapidly advanced over the years to a point where there is a fair amount of headroom for graphical detail to exist in a game environment. ... [I]s the world presented [in a given video game] about stopping and pondering nature, savoring a detail level that has moss growing from antipodean directions to the sun? Or is the game all about

getting the player to the next joy trigger as smoothly and deftly as possible, with just enough detail to keep the focal beats strung together? Are both extremes to be accommodated, if not equally appeased?

9.3 Meaningful Experience

Findings suggest that gamers may demonstrate more advanced visual-selective attention skills and 'superior abilities in several attention-related tasks compared with non-gamers' to a statistically significant degree, 'suggesting that video game playing has beneficial effects on the player' in cognitive terms (Matern et al., 2019: 6–8), which in the context of our study highlights the potential of meaningful cognitive and experiential phenomena related to gaming. For instance, a paper by Nacke and Lindley (2010: 1) argues that 'clear and testable definitions' of constructs relating to subjective player experiences 'would be invaluable for game designers, since they are considered to be the holy grail of digital game design'. This brings us to an overarching question about the meaning of games.

Crucially however, the term 'games' attempts to encompass a vast (and ever-growing) set of very different interactive and multimodal phenomena. Thus, one perspective on the medium is that of ludic play. The editorial by Musselwhite and colleagues (2016: 2), for instance, scrutinises the idea that play is 'unnecessary, discretionary' and instead advances the belief that 'to live is to play', arguing that 'informality, curiosity and humor' – all well exemplified, for example, by *SW2* – are aspects not at all insignificant to 'a truly fulfilled life'. Another perspective would acknowledge the aspirations of certain titles to leverage the potential of an interactive new medium to perhaps transcend informality, becoming yet more intricate, art-like and ostensibly serious – not unlike *TCTD2*. Either way, the traditionally common view that games are a superficial form of unsophisticated entertainment seems to be seen more and more as a misconception (see Section 2.2.1) even by individuals who do not engage with games in a professional, scholarly or leisurely fashion. Along these lines, Paul (2014: 459) opens his chapter by succinctly stating that '(v)ideo games matter'. He goes on to expound that they 'mean something to the people who play them, the designers and companies that produce them, and the cultures in which they are made and played', then arguing for three categories of meaning: 'the meaning of games, the meaning in games, and the meaning created around games and game culture' (459).

We also asked Mazur about the notion of 'exclusivity' in OSL in audiovisual media in general, especially in relation to the backgrounded elements. These elements may become liminal in terms of perceptibility, yet carry potential to transform the playing/viewing experience for those able to spot them, which in a sense creates a rather ludic relation between the creation and its recipients (i.e. challenging them in order to 'unlock' further content). He related it to environmental storytelling, while also adding:

> I think such procedures are brilliant. We try to incorporate those in our games, too . . . . But I need to remind you that *SW2* is action-driven. Such elements are unimportant. There are plot-driven games where such a procedure would be more appropriate. But we do use it.

We wish to posit that OSL, especially its liminally prominent instantiations, contributes to the meaning of a game in valuable ways. The very property of limited accessibility of these visual stimuli constitutes their value, all the more because that property is introduced intentionally by the creators, which need not always be the case when such elements appear in films where chance can play a role. The players who are able to retrieve these elements have the opportunity to construct additional meanings and appreciate the effort of the game creators. At the same time, we should keep it in mind that players differ, which can be consequential in at least two ways. First, players will be differently likely to register cases of liminal OSL in games. Second, once registered, liminal cases of OSL will be more or less positively evaluated depending on several parameters ranging from the player's background knowledge – not limited to games – to psychological considerations like individual differences and personality.

9.3.1 Player Preferences and Sources of Motivation

This links to the idea of play-style and player motivation. Both of these concepts have been indirectly referenced in Sections 4.2 and 4.3, describing the specificities of the research-oriented play-through of the two games studied in this Element, implying there is more than one way to play through a single game. It may seem even natural for an interactive medium, after all. In the case of the play-through in question, considering its key-component of slower-paced, careful exploration, which evidently skewed the playtime in comparison to the average play-throughs indicated in the case of both games, it presumably differed greatly from the 'usual' game experience of the two titles.

However, that is not to say *exploration* is not a vital component of the default expectation of players. It is interpreted as one quadrant of the four basic gameplay preferences, alongside *socialising, killing* (dominating) and *achievement-seeking*, in a model proposed in 1996 to taxonomise the profiles of an MUD-type game (offering multi-user worlds, typically for role-playing) players (Bartle, 1996). Another instance of its inclusion is as one of five primary dimensions recognised in the meta-synthesis of player-type models (Hamari & Tuunanen, 2014):

exploration, achievement, immersion, sociability and *domination,* alongside other typology propositions, such as gaming *intensity* and *in-game demographics.*

Understanding the differences in player preferences or the sources of motivation, and what that can entail in a multiplayer setting, may be pivotal for the development of nuanced VGs. In *TCTD2,* for example, the dev team provided an option to the player to display the play-style they are inclined towards, from a range of pre-selected combinations, to show to other players during guild/clan matchmaking. These include: *player versus player, player versus environment, relaxed atmosphere, hardcore atmosphere, focused atmosphere, accessibility-features, parenting, achievement hunting, competitive, content creation, role-playing, cosplaying, single-playing, socialising, guide-creation/newcomer support, lore-uncovering* as well as *inclusive* and *no* preferences. The list is certainly elaborate; however it still could be expanded.

Suggestions for this may concentrate on vastly different approaches to the topic than the established, aforementioned ones. For example, the utilitary conceptual framework by Tondello and colleagues (2017) proposes at least nine groups of game element proclivity and five groups of styles. These are: *management, puzzle-solving, art appreciation, sport and skill, role-playing, virtual good acquisition, simulation, action* and *progression,* and *multiplayer, abstract interactions, solo play, competitive play* and *casual play,* respectively. Similarly, worth noting are the heuristics for recognised multifaceted gaming mentalities – based, among other things, on *space, genre, access, intensity* and *commitment* of the game and gamers – and the proposed 'at least' nine reasons/ ways to play – including, with some overlap: being able to share games in a social setting, killing time and just experiencing the game, as 'gaming is important in itself' (Kallio et al., 2011: 329–39).

As mentioned in Sections 2.2.1 and 2.4.1, there are also less per segaming-oriented reasons to utilise VGs, which is exemplified by the para-gaming socio-cultural and socio-political as well as creative movements (e.g. the machinima community). Moreover, they see use in simulation, medicine, research and education (e.g. language-learning; cf. Aguilar et al., 2015).

9.3.2 Minimising the Mismatch of Player Experience

To argue that untranslated OSL creates potential for cross-cultural and cross-linguistic meaning construction and experience asymmetry is just the first step. For the purposes of translation, the context in which they appear has paramount importance, given their different relationships to the game world and their ensuing functionality.

A natural question is then about the available localisation solutions for cases of OSL in games. An optimal solution could be to offer translation in the form of subtitle-like text displayed on screen. However, the text would need to be displayed upon the player's intentional action, that is the player would need to notice the case of OSL to be able to activate its contextual translation. That has the advantage of requiring the player to visually register OSL and choose to invest effort to process it, rather than having the translation displayed by default and therefore being put in a privileged position in relation to the English-speaking players. This solution has the disadvantage of incurring the additional effort of activating the translation, for example by clicking on the element, which is not required of the player who speaks the SL. Another disadvantage is that the translation would be visually superimposed, that is, it would stand out as external to the game's world, which could be drawing attention to the mediating presence of translation and likely detracting from the realistic immersive experience.

Nonetheless, that is the approach taken by the developers/localisation team of the third-person-perspective graphic-adventure game *Life is Strange* (2015), where akin to older point-and-click or isometric role-playing computer games, some instances of OSL – those made interactive – when selected by the player, can be viewed from a first-person perspective and up-close, but only in an original, untranslated state. At the same time, a specially designated transcribing button appears in the corner of the screen. Upon activation of this function, any verbal contents of the visual asset are displayed on the screen in pure text format on top of the original asset, synthesising both the textual content and graphical form. This pure text can then be localised on a per-locale basis. This solution has the added benefit of optimising the gameplay for any player who might choose to play the game with the textures being rendered in lower quality – in some cases making text blurry and uncomfortable to read – so as to run the game on a hardware unable to optimally run it otherwise. The ability to read OSLs regardless of the capabilities of the computer on which the game is being run can be quite consequential in this case. Arguably, the core gameplay loop (cycles of actions designed to engage the player) of *Life is Strange* majorly consists of inspecting interactive objects for their textual information provided on, or alongside them. Moreover, the protagonist often remarks on the content or context of the inspected in-game asset, and sometimes reads aloud its verbal elements, which is then subtitled and could even be dubbed. Such 'localisation-devices-turned accessibility-features'[48] seem to be an established sight in VGs

---

[48] Bernal-Merino (2020: 308) likewise assesses that accessibility functionalities are provided by the same teams that are tasked with localisation: 'It is the language service providers that inform and deliver most of the accessibility features once game companies integrate such design changes.'

revolving around world-building and storytelling, as elaborated on in Section 2.5.2.

We consulted Mazur on the ways to make such elements more accessible to those reliant on localisation to process the in-game texts. Among other things, we asked if it would be possible to implement a system in which an interactable contextual menu with translation of (especially) non-string OSL could pop up at the designated location or if it would be better to leave those elements for the players to translate themselves. He answered:

> That's interesting. I've never thought about it. Another linguistic issue is that some texts would be difficult to transfer/communicate in localisation. I wonder how it's being done in more story-driven games. I don't think those are considered decoration there. I don't remember seeing any of that, though. I think they would be more plot-related. Then they'll be translated, too.

Another solution is embedding translation graphically as part of the game's world, which could seem a more immersive alternative. However, such extreme domestication or adaptation would clearly be ruled out in the case of games explicitly set in a particular culture and language. In the case of *TCTD2*, the action explicitly takes place in the United States, which motivates the use of English in the OSL. Substituting Polish text for the original would result in major inconsistencies as posters, notices, names of institutions and products across Washington would be worded in a language other than the convention-ally expected one. A VG localisation implementing this approach is a point-and-click graphic adventure game *Sam & Max: Season One* (2006). Its comedic setting and at times nonsensical humour, starring the titular anthropomorphic dog and rabbit protagonist detective duo, may have influenced the decision to 'polonise' (some portions of) the OSL, practically incorporating the TL into the presented world, which is otherwise clearly inspired by the past-century New York City.

In terms of *SW2*, Mazur acknowledged the possibility and suggested ways to graphically localise non-string OSL, but remained sceptical whether that is always a go-to solution:

> Probably there are some technical means to do this. One could just make a texture like that from the ground up. A non-string OSL is as if painted on the graphic. So when the texture's file doesn't have layers [e.g. one for the 'background' image itself and one for the graphic text], you can't just delete the text [without deleting the texture, too].

One could also graphically blur the text and write on top of it – however questions might be raised regarding the quality of the effect produced by such a solution. Mazur added as follows:

Anticipating that, you could prepare the assets using complex file formats, where you can create separate layers for all this, so that later just the text can be edited. But I've never seen this being done, I think. There were situations in which our 2D graphics artist had to remaster textures, but rather to repair some mistake [i.e. not in the context of standardised localisation]. Already then we learnt that this is not a viable option.

Thus there is also the question of technical limitations to that approach, especially when it comes to older games. Such efforts would technically fall into the category referred to as *asset management*, or in this case per-culture asset substitution, in contrast to *text localisation*. Both are, for example, evidently functionally available for utilisation in the localisation suite of Unreal engine-based VGs.[49] However, it is said that *TCTD2* is based on the Snowdrop game engine (likewise, *SW2* is based on an in-house Road Hog game engine), which without programmer-confirmation makes it difficult to assert if such an option was even possible, yet alone considered.

9.4 Towards 'Accessible Gamedev'?

A productive framework for thinking about game development and game localisation could be constructed by extending Romero-Fresco's (2013) proposal of 'accessible filmmaking' (AFM). Starting from the observation (Romero-Fresco 2020: 545) that the standard had been for translation to be conceived of as 'an afterthought', a process 'involving zero contact with the creative team', Romero-Fresco (2019) argues for an approach where translation, or more broadly accessibility provision services, are integrated already into the media production stage, thus challenging the 'industrialised model that relegates accessibility and translation to the distribution process' (Romero-Fresco 2020: 561).

On a practical plane, that critically encompasses collaboration between the translator and the creative team, which has already been attested (e.g. Romero-Fresco, 2020: 557–8; Zanotti, 2018) but is far from standard. While such collaboration will to some extent alter the professional practices for all the parties involved, it will be mutually beneficial. First, as Romero-Fresco observes, from the perspective of the original creators:

The aim here is not to compromise the filmmakers' vision or constrain their freedom, but rather to reveal to them often unknown aspects of how their films are changed in their translated and accessible versions. AFM presents them with different options so that they can make choices that determine the

---

[49] See Epic Games, Inc. (n.d.), particularly the 'Asset Localization' and 'Text Localization' sections.

nature of these translated/accessible versions. Until now, these choices were made exclusively by the translator or the distributor. Rather than compromising the filmmakers' vision, this collaboration will help to preserve it across different audiences.

Then, conversely, from the vantage point of the translator, AFM allows for a more informed decision-making process whereby any mismatches between the original and its accessible as well as translated versions are minimised while critically keeping track of the filmmakers' vision.

Following this line of reasoning, we wish to propose that new prospects for translation, but also accessibility beyond linguacultural barriers, could be opened if the approach is taken even further. The proposal is to consider translation and accessibility when the audiovisual product – in our case, the game – is still under development. A like-minded view of AFM's potential in wider contexts is voiced by Romero-Fresco, with special focus on sensory impairment and theatrical performances. That view – perhaps somewhat tellingly given in a footnote (Romero-Fresco 2020: 558) – is as follows:

> Interestingly, AFM can also be regarded as part of a wider movement aiming to integrate translation and accessibility as part of the artistic creation process. The theatre is proving particularly active in this regard, with examples such as *The Gift*, a play produced by the professional Northern Irish children's touring theatre company Cahoots NI in 2015 (Maguire, 2015). With the help of the researcher Tom Maguire, the production of the play included aspects of universal design early on in the process and in collaboration with the creative team in order to ensure that spectators with visual impairment were as integrated in the play as sighted spectators.

When it comes to VG localisation practices, that approach does not (yet?) seem to be deployed with interlingual and cross-cultural considerations in mind when it comes to OSL. At the same time, there is already a fair degree of recognition of the position of language in the multisemiotic set-up of VGs. Such a view of the current gamedev trends is voiced by Bernal-Merino (2020) who observes that 'many interactive entertainment companies (e.g. the Polish CD Projekt Red) are starting to embrace' such a business model (310), whereby 'localised versions are produced almost in absolute parallel with the original' (298). Most importantly, however, he exemplifies how theory already meets practice, describing how the implementation of the 'glocalisation strategy' can influence the quality and sales of such products (307–12). For instance, he points out that the team behind the critically acclaimed *The Witcher 3* 'worked with translation agencies to make sure that they preserved playability and the unique adventure style of the game' across locales (309). Nonetheless, on the whole, the industry is far from fully adopting such a model:

The move of some game localisation processes from the postproduction stage at the very end of product development to the planning stages constitutes a radical change requiring serious restructuring in most game companies as many of them had organically become accustomed to disregarding the preferences of foreign markets, owing to the fact that outsourced language service providers would undertake this part of the work at a later stage. ... The glocalisation strategy signals a shift in which localisation becomes closely involved with video game creation, effectively generating new versions of the game .... One of the most decisive factors determining this enhanced localisation approach ... is that these products are conceived from the very beginning as global mass market consumer products, and not as canonical works of art, as some literary and filmic creations are regarded nowadays. (310)

Michał Mazur of Flying Wild Hog pointed out that at his studio, the writers of the original language version indeed collaborate with other members of the development team in a way that ensures space for negotiation. The designers are thus willing to revise their original ideas to better accommodate the language component – for example, adjustments can be made in the amount of time or space allocated to a particular case of language use in the game, whether implemented in the audio or visual layer, if brought up early enough during the development. Still, that is the case with the original – mostly English – version of the game, which is motivated by practical considerations of market size. A step further would be to keep in mind the language- and culture-specific constraints of other markets to be better suited to minimise the asymmetry of player experience as games are distributed globally.

9.5 The (Research) Potential of In-Game OSL

When it comes to further avenues of inquiry, a characteristic of the methodology we have utilised for this Element is that it draws on manual and interpretation-driven analysis. Leaving aside its markedly labour- and time-intensive character, it comes with a degree of subjectivity, even if measures are taken to minimise it, such as collaboration – involving two researchers in our case. To further systematise OSL in a translation perspective, a future study may utilise a localised version of an offline-only game with open-source programming code to extract all game textures from the game's files, selecting the instances of OSL and categorising them quantitatively based on features like how many of the instances have been translated into the target language. A further step would be to factor in the dimensions of function and prominence. That research could employ (large-scale online) questionnaires as well as verbal protocols, and a range of physiological measures to probe reception, with eye-tracking appearing particularly well-suited to investigate player processing of OSL. Such an empirically grounded reception perspective is still emerging (cf. e.g. Mangiron, 2018: 292) and it neatly corresponds with the proposal of 'user-centered translation' (O'Hagan, 2019: 153; Suojanen et al. 2015) as well as proactive user-centric postulates and solutions from audiovisual translation and media accessibility (Greco, 2018; Romero-Fresco, 2019; see also Section 9.4). In-game OSL could therefore serve as a proxy for expanding our understanding of how players engage with games across language versions.

By way of conclusion, let us consider the following point by Bishop (2018: 10):

> Video games, by their very nature, are intensely visual creations, and the artists who create these games necessarily spend long hours determining exactly what their players will see. There is no happenchance in the visual field of such a game, no random or thoughtless inconsistencies. Everything that appears before the player has been designed and set in place – landscapes are designed, scripts are written, and actors are paid to perform their lines. It is with this in mind that we should review even the most (apparently) minor detail.

This conceptualisation of VGs highlights the significance of in-game OSL and – given the global nature of VG distribution – brings into the equation the translational facet. The Element has therefore aspired to highlight in-game OSL as an under-explored layer of VGs. With their variable cognitive status and multiple underlying mechanisms, OSL brings great meaning-making potential and can cause significant cross-linguistic and cross-cultural player experience mismatches. These mismatches need to be addressed in the context of VG localisation to truly maximise the analogousness of access to content globally.

Appendix

Narrative inscriptions documented throughout the play-through of *Tom Clancy's The Division 2* (282 in total):

(GROUP 1): 'True DC', 'Washington needs to rise up', 'We are stronger than a government that abonded [sic] us', 'where is our aid?', 'help the people in need', 'we say NO and demand MORE', 'RIP THE SYSTEM', 'kick the crap out of all this B.S.', 'C.E.R.A. FAILED', 'fukk [sic] them!', 'you are a GRENADE against the government', 'love is still a winner', 'we are FISH out of water jumping for air', 'virus is a punishment', 'piles of joy', 'air f(a)rce gone', 'living in the shadow of the monument', 'wake up sheep', 'usa is fukked [sic]', 'fuck the government', 'world is broke [sic]', 'boom cu(o)p [sic] the govmnt [sic]', 'we need new leaders new powers', 'we will rise', 'ucan't [sic] break Washington', 'we have rights', 'yo, yo, now its low life bum life for all in the capital', 'I love Anthony', 'go big', 'not the time for TEMPER', 'virus nation', 'blow out', 'act now government! stop screwing us!', 'washington [illegible] up!', 'fix WSH NOW', 'where is order & law?!', 'wasted state', 'peace through strength', 'the virus is a hoax', 'CLUB OF SHEEP', 'wake up and take back DC', 'GOV KILLS US', 'sup it [illegible]', 'RAD rules all!', 'a for anarchy', 'love & [illegible]', 'RELAX YOURSELF', 'fuck you get out!','WSH is still Alive!', 'UNITE', 'what a time to be alive!', 'DC IS DEAD', 'welcome to shitville', 'boat! race! bitches!', 'give us some love', 'FKKK [sic] C.E.R.A.', 'FKKK [sic] the state', 'Rogue little fkrz [sic]', 'virus 4 all', 'sukz [sic]', 'suck it', 'slip it in', 'ORLY FU [sic]', 'dunk it!', 'RIP rip WSH DC', 'This is OUR land', 'killonsight', 'WE HAVE MORE GUNS THAN YOU', 'IF YOU CAN READ THIS YOU ARE DEAD', 'HELP US', 'OUR RIGHTS OUR COUNTRY IF YOU DON'T HELP US YOU MUST FALL', 'WE DEMAND VACCINES! OUR LIFES [sic] ARE IMPORTANT TOO', 'VACCINES NOW!', 'ANGRY SIGN' [sic!], 'BRING BACK ORDER', 'FKKK THIS BS [sic] THE ELITE GET VACCINES WE DON'T', 'supplies and water PLEASE !', 'this is -NOT-ok', 'ENOUGH! Where is CERA where is the aid?', 'ACT NOW GOVERNMENT STOP [illegible]!', 'PROTECT YOUR CITIZENS', 'FUCK OFF AND DIE', 'DC! RISE!', 'you wont [sic] let us live we won't let you rule RESIST', 'WAKE UP AMERICA take back wsh', 'everything looks like a gun from here', 'rights, hope, unity, reality', 'NO', 'X', 'DC: GOOD LUCK OUT THERE', 'WSH IS NR1', 'FU', 'ffs [sic] give us a vaccine', 'clean up'.

(GROUP 2): 'no tomorrow END OF THE WORLD PARTY infected welcome', 'end of the world party no tomorrow!! 9PM-ETERNITY!',

'HELP!', 'outsiders will be shot', 'stay out', 'world', 'NO free handouts', 'DO NOT ENTER', 'ENTRANCE', 'WALK AWAY', 'don't waste', 'clean!!', 'dead inside', 'storage area', 'keep moving, no idling', 'J.T.F.', 'J.T.F.-A.H.S.', 'low security', 'high security', 'clan quarters', 'rally point', 'looters will be SHOT', 'rule breakers will be punished', 'last warning!', 'welcome', 'checkpoint', 'quartermaster', 'stay in lane', 'speaker of da house', 'test subjects', 'WARNING residents only', 'food here', 'drink', 'take what you need', 'disinfect, use MINIMUM amount (And wash hands!)', 'we were betrayed', 'OURS NOW', 'authorized personnel only', 'Welcome To Historic District', 'enjoy your meal!', 'this week's food menu: 1. grilled chicken & salad 2. vegetable mix & soy 'burgers' 3. hamburgers with bacon 4. caesar salad 5. rice & pork 6. soup deluxe with fresh baked bread and our own butter 7. fish dish deluxe, juice, milk, softdrinks, water, tea, sparkling water to drink', 'entrance', 'keep clear, make way', 'clothes here', 'water here', 'BOOZE', 'provisions here', 'keep closed', 'help yourself', 'WE HAVE GUNS!', 'ammo here', 'medical bay', 'workshop', 'do NOT touch', 'assembly', 'arena', 'food hall', 'dormitory', 'DON'T leave it on!', 'PACK YOUR BED', 'PAINKILLERS take ONE', 'collection point', 'leisure space here', 'DRUG', 'drink drink drink', 'private', 'gambling', 'boss room, boss only!', 'take care of this', 'garage', 'stockpile', 'kindergarten', 'packing', 'drug kitchen', 'GUARD DUTY: group A: 12AM → 6AM, B: 6AM → 12PM, C: 12PM → 6PM, D: 6PM → 12AM', 'Do Not Drink Do Not Drink', 'DRYER', 'trash', 'SUPPLIES', 'DEATH AWAITS', 'bulletproof', 'barracks', 'comms2', 'h1', 'h2', 'h3', 'hesco', 'front', 'docks (heli)', 'hesco???', 'antiviral prio!!', 'ER ROOM', 'INFIRMARY', 'BRIEFING ROOM', 'OPERATIONS ROOM', 'dog food', '-1', '-2 you are HERE', '-3 metro', 'silo', 'floration room', 'WORK OR DIE', 'FREIGHT ONLY', 'vendor', 'patrol routes', 'west: 01 SPI FZ > 04 SAN MI > 08 SAN KIRIN, east: [etc.]', 'CONEY ISLAND', 'explosives here', 'drop-off point', 'missile parts here', 'to be moved (do not stack), 'need food & water', 'keep calm', 'days to evac: 1', 'SOLAR PARK', 'REDACTED', 'emergency team officer'.

(GROUP 3): 'levelhead? [sic]', 'USA', 'LISA+JG', 'freak in [sic] chaos', 'killing time', 'sleep', 'greed [illegible]', 'sweet', 'a sweet tonic wasta [sic]', 'funky', 'quiet', 'relax', 'ruckus', 'bro', 'king', 'HOAX', 'CHECK 1–2', 'C.H. F.F. is BOGUS', 'WASHINGTON BLAZING BOOGIE', 'kick it', 'shrimp', 'war', 'Cyrez', 'johnson28', 'funisher', 'santi', 'groove', 'grind', 'meow', 'POF', 'ABA', 'MOB', 'RAM', 'THEM', 'switcharo' [sic], 'DC TANKS', 'OUT', 'resho', 'uzurp [sic]', 'BYMZ', 'safe', 'deus ex ae[illegible]', 'xyz', '$', '#', 'KS', 'MISFITZ' [sic], 'rollojoy', 'underdog', 'shank', 'brainwash', 'broke life', 'ebe', 'hobo haven', 'sc part funk' and a number of other illegible 'throw-up tags'.

References

3D Realms (1991–2010). *Duke Nukem* series [Game]. 3D Realms.

3D Realms (1997–2013). *Shadow Warrior* series [Games]. 3D Realms.

Aguilar, S. J., Holman, C. & Fishman, B. J. (2015). 'Game-Inspired Design: Empirical Evidence in Support of Gameful Learning Environments'. *Games and Culture*, 13(1), 44–70. https://doi.org/10.1177/1555412015600305.

Amick, T., Long, G., Schell, J. & Shehan, G. (2015). 'A History of Video Game Consoles'. IST final report. https://sites.psu.edu/gshehan/wp-content/uploads/sites/24736/2015/03/IST110_Final_Report.pdf. Accessed 15 August 2021.

Antonelli, P. (2012). 'Video Games: 14 in the Collection, for Starters'. New York: Museum of Modern Art. www.moma.org/explore/inside_out/2012/11/29/video-games-14-in-the-collection-for-starters/. Accessed 15 September 2021.

Badstübner-Kizik, C. (2019). 'Multilingualism in the Movies: Languages in Films Revisited'. In M. Deckert (ed.), *Audiovisual Translation: Research and Use* (2nd ed.). Berlin: Peter Lang, 246–67.

Bareither, C. (2020). *Playful Virtual Violence: An Ethnography of Emotional Practices in Video Games*. Elements in Histories of Emotions and the Senses. Cambridge: Cambridge University Press.

Bareja, S. (dir.) (1980). *Miś* [Teddy Bear]. Zespół Filmowy 'Perspektywa'.

Bartle, R. (1996). 'Hearts, Clubs, Diamonds, Spaced: Players Who Suit MUDs'. *The Journal of Virtual Entertainments*, 1, 19. https://mud.co.uk/richard/hcds.htm.

Bavelier, D., Achtman, R. L., Mani, M. & Föcker, J. (2012). 'Neural Bases of Selective Attention in Action Video Game Players'. *Vision Research*, 61, 132–43. https://doi.org/10.1016/j.visres.2011.08.007.

'Bethesda Ruins' (n.d.). Nukapedia Fallout Wiki. https://fallout.fandom.com/wiki/Bethesda_ruins. Accessed 18 September 2021.

Bernal-Merino, M. Á. (2006). 'On the Translation of Video Games'. *The Journal of Specialised Translation*, 6, 22–36. www.jostrans.org/issue06.

Bernal-Merino, M. Á. (2007). 'What's in a "Game"?'. *Localisation Focus: The International Journal of Localisation*, 6(1), 29–39.

Bernal-Merino, M. Á. (2013). *The Localisation of Video Games*. Doctoral thesis, Imperial College London. https://doi.org/10.25560/39333.

Bernal-Merino, M. Á. (2015). *Translation and Localisation in Video Games: Making Entertainment Software Global* (1st ed.). New York: Routledge.

Bernal-Merino, M. Á. (2016). 'Creating Felicitous Gaming Experiences: Semiotics and Pragmatics as Tools for Video Game Localisation'. *Signata*, 7(1), 231–53. https://doi.org/10.4000/signata.1227.

Bernal-Merino, M. Á. (2018). 'Quantum Identity and the Enhancement of Communication'. *Journal of Brand Strategy*, 6(4), 380–91.

Bernal-Merino, M. Á. (2020). 'Key Concepts in Game Localisation Quality'. In M. Deckert & Ł. Bogucki (eds.), *The Palgrave Handbook of Audiovisual Translation and Media Accessibility*. Cham: Palgrave Macmillan, 297–315.

Berry, N. (2015). 'The Difficulties of Open World Design'. *Making Games*, 6, 56–63. https://s3-eu-west-1.amazonaws.com/editor.production.pressmatrix .com/emags/210770/pdfs/original/d87229ab-f70b-4755-80d7-52ffe006423e .pdf. Accessed 26 September 2022.

Bethesda Game Studios (2008). *Fallout 3* [Game]. Bethesda Softworks.

Bishop, C. (2018). 'Reading Antiquity in Metro Redux'. *Games and Culture*, 15(3), 1–20. https://doi.org/10.1177/1555412018786649.

Bleichenbacher, L. (2008). *Multilingualism in the Movies: Hollywood Characters and Their Language Choices*. Tübingen: Franke Verlag.

Blizzard Entertainment & Iron Galaxy. (2016). *Overwatch*. [Game]. Blizzard Entertainment.

Bogost, I. (2006). 'Playing Politics: Videogames for Politics, Activism, and Advocacy'. *First Monday*. https://doi.org/10.5210/fm.v0i0.1617.

Bogucki, Ł. (2013). *Areas and Methods of Audiovisual Translation Research* (3rd ed.). Berlin: Peter Lang.

Bogucki, Ł. (2016). 'Rendering Otherness in Film: Techniques for Translating Multilingual Audiovisual Material'. In B. Lewandowska-Tomaszczyk, M. Thelen, G.-W. van Egdom, D. Verbeeck & Ł. Bogucki (eds.), *Translation and Meaning New Series*, vol. 1. Frankfurt: Peter Lang, 183–91.

Bohannon, J. (2014). 'Online Video Game Plugs Players into Remote-Controlled Biochemistry Lab'. *Science*, 343(6170), 475. https://doi.org/10.1126/science .343.6170.475.

Campbell, C. (2019). 'Death Stranding's Product Placement Is an Act of Vandalism'. Polygon. www.polygon.com/2019/11/14/20955496/death-stranding-monster-energy-product-placement-kojima. Accessed 6 September 2021.

Camper, B. B. (2005). 'Homebrew and the Social Construction of Gaming: Community, Creativity, and Legal Context of Amateur Game Boy Advance Development'. Master's thesis, Massachusetts Institute of Technology. https://dspace.mit.edu/handle/1721.1/42227.

CD Projekt Red, Tomaszkiewicz, K., Kanik, M. et al. (2015). *The Witcher 3: Wild Hunt* [Game].

Chabris, C. F. & Simons, D. J. (2010). *The Invisible Gorilla*. London: Crown Publishers.

Chiaro, D. (2010). 'Found in Translation: Crosstalk as a Form of Humour'. In C. Valero-Garcés (ed.), *Dimensions of Humor: Explorations in Linguistics, Literature, Cultural Studies and Translation*. Valencia: University of Valencia Press, 33–54.

Chiaro, D. & De Bonis, G. (2020). 'Multilingualism and Translation on Screen'. In Ł. Bogucki & M. Deckert (eds.), *The Palgrave Handbook of Audiovisual Translation and Media Accessibility*. Cham: Palgrave Macmillan, 687–711.

Clancy, T. (n.d.). 'Red Storm Entertainment Press Releases'. Red Storm. https://accessed:archive.org/web/19970629052550/http://www.redstorm.com/press releases.html. Accessed 31 August 2022.

'Clock Puzzle' (n.d.). Silent Hill Wiki. https://silenthill.fandom.com/wiki/Clock_Puzzle. Accessed 14 September 2020.

Copenhaver, A. (2014). 'Violent Video Game Legislation as Pseudo-agenda'. *Criminal Justice Studies*, 28(2), 170–85. https://doi.org/10.1080/1478601x.2014.966474.

Culture.pl (n.d.). 'O nas'. ['About Us']. Adam Mickiewicz Institute. https://culture.pl/pl/o-nas. Accessed 14 April 2022.

Culture.pl (2016). '"Post-Post-Modern Gaming"? An Interview with Flying Wild Hog'. Culture.pl. 10 November. https://culture.pl/en/article/post-post-modern-gaming-an-interview-with-flying-wild-hog. Accessed 26 August 2022.

Deckert, M. (2021). 'Język w przestrzeni ekranu: przekładowe nieoczywiste oczywistości'. In P. Stalmaszczyk (ed.), *Język(i) w czasie i przestrzeni*. Lodz: Lodz University Press, 99–114.

Deckert, M. & Jaszczyk, P. (2019). 'Subtitling Choices and Visual Attention: A Viewer Perspective'. In P. Pietrzak (ed.), *New Insights into Translator Training* (special issue). *inTRAlinea*. https://intralinea.org/specials/article/2414.

deHaan, J. (2019). 'Teaching Language and Literacy with Games: What? How? Why?' *Ludic Language Pedagogy*, 1, 1–57. https://llpjournal.org/2019/09/18/dehaan-what-how-why.html.

Derrat, M. (2021). 'Top 10 Most Profound Games Ever Made'. YouTube video. https://youtu.be/kwlGiLuRBB8/.

Desimone, R. & Duncan, J. (1995). 'Neural Mechanisms of Selective Visual Attention'. *Annual Review of Neuroscience*, 18, 193–222.

Dietz, F. (2006). 'Issues in Localizing Computer Games'. In K. Dunne (ed.), *Perspectives on Localization*. Amsterdam: John Benjamins, 121–34.

Dillio, R. (2014). 'A Critical Miss: Video Games, Violence, and Ineffective Legislation'. *First Amendment Studies*, 48(2), 110–30. https://doi.org/10.1080/21689725.2014.950496.

Dontnod Entertainment (2015). *Life Is Strange* [Game]. Square Enix Europe.

Dunne, K. J. (2006). 'Issues in Localizing Computer Games'. In K. J. Dunne (ed.), *Perspectives on Localization*. Amsterdam: John Benjamins, 121–34.

Epic Games, Inc. (n.d.). 'Localization'. Unreal Engine 5.0 documentation. https://docs.unrealengine.com/5.0/en-US/localizing-content-in-unreal-engine-for-different-cultures/. Accessed 17 September 2021.

Ferguson, C. J., & Colwell, J. (2017). 'Understanding Why Scholars Hold Different Views on the Influences of Video Games on Public Health'. *Journal of Communication*, 67(3), 305–27. https://doi.org/10.1111/jcom.12293.

Ferguson, C. J., & Wang, J. C. K. (2019). 'Aggressive Video Games Are Not a Risk Factor for Future Aggression in Youth: A Longitudinal Study'. *Journal of Youth and Adolescence*, 48(8), 1439–51. https://doi.org/10.1007/s10964-019-01069-0.

Fernandez-Vara, C. (2011). 'Game Spaces Speak Volumes: Indexical Storytelling'. *Proceedings of the 2011 DiGRA International Conference: Think Design Play*. DiGRA/Utrecht School of Arts. www.digra.org/wp-content/uploads/digital-library/Game-Spaces-Speak-Volumes.pdf.

Fisher, S. J. & Harvey, A. (2013). 'Intervention for Inclusivity: Gender Politics and Indie Game Development'. *Loading... The Journal of the Canadian Game Studies Association*, 7(11). https://loading.journals.publicknowledge project.org/loading/index.php/loading/article/view/118/183.

Fleming, V. (dir.) (1939). *The Wizard of Oz*. Loew's, Inc.

Flying Wild Hog. (2011). *Hard Reset* [Game]. Flying Wild Hog & Good Shepherd Entertainment.

Flying Wild Hog. (2014). *Juju* [Game]. Flying Wild Hog.

Flying Wild Hog. (2016). *Shadow Warrior 2* [Game]. Devolver Digital.

Fredricksen, E. (2002) *Progress Quest* [Game]. http://fredricksen.net/.

Fullbright Company (2013). *Gone Home* [Game].

Gambier, Y. (2003). 'Introduction: Screen Transadaptation: Perception and Reception'. *The Translator*, 9(2), 171–89. https://doi.org/10.1080/13556509.2003.10799152.

GDC (2018a). 'A Fun Time in Which Some No-Good Game Developers May or May Not Discuss How We Made NieR:Automata'. YouTube video. https://youtu.be/jKbH9i5axxU. Accessed 27 September 2021.

GDC (2018b). 'Failing to Fail: The Spiderweb Software Way'. YouTube video. http://youtu.be/stxVBJem3Rs. Accessed 21 August 2021.

Gee, J. P. (2005). *Why Video Games Are Good for Your Soul: Pleasure and Learning*. Melbourne: Common Ground Publishing.

Gee, J. P. (2006). 'Why Game Studies Now? Video Games: A New Art Form'. *Games and Culture*, 1(1), 58–61. https://doi.org/10.1177/155541200 5281788.

Greco, G. M. (2018). 'The Nature of Accessibility Studies'. *Journal of Audiovisual Translation*, 1(1), 205–32.

Griffiths, M. (2005). 'Video Games and Health'. *British Medical Journal*, 331(7509), 122–3. https://doi.org/10.1136/bmj.331.7509.122.

Hall, L., Johansson, P., Tarning, B., Sikstrom, S. & Deutgen, T. (2010). 'Magic at the Marketplace: Choice Blindness for the Taste of Jam and the Smell of Tea'. *Cognition*, 117(1), 54–61.

Hamari, J. & Tuunanen, J. (2014). Player Types: A Meta-synthesis. *DIGRA: Transactions of the Digital Games Research Association*, 1(2), 29–53. http://dx.doi.org/10.26503/todigra.v1i2.13.

Harvey, A. & Fisher, S. (2014). '"Everyone Can Make Games!": The Postfeminist Context of Women in Digital Game Production'. *Feminist Media Studies*, 15(4), 576–92. https://doi.org/10.1080/14680777.2014.958867.

Hazelton, R. (2014). 'Learning the Poetic Line'. Poetry Foundation. www.poetry foundation.org/articles/70144/learning-the-poetic-line. Accessed 9 May 2021.

Hempuli & Teikari, A. (2019). *Baba Is You* [Game]. Hempuli.

Henry, J. (2019). 'The Division 2 Devs Reveal Story Length'. Gamer Rant. 18 January. www.gamerant.com/division-2-story-length. Accessed 26 August 2022.

International Trade Administration. (2020). 'Media & Entertainment'. International Trade Administration, United States Department of Commerce. www.trade.gov/media-entertainment/. Accessed 25 August 2021.

International Trade Administration (n.d.). 'Media & Entertainment: Video Games Sector'. International Trade Administration, United States Department of Commerce. www.trade.gov/media-entertainment-video-games sector. Accessed 25 August 2021.

Interplay, Black Isle Studios, Bethesda & Obsidian (1997–present). *Fallout* series [Games].

'In the Studio'. (1997). *Next Generation*, 26 (February), 34. https://archive.org/details/nextgen-issue-26/page/n35/mode/2up.

Izushi, H. & Aoyama, Y. (2006). 'Industry Evolution and Cross-Sectoral Skill Transfers: A Comparative Analysis of the Video Game Industry in Japan, the United States, and the United Kingdom'. *Environment and Planning A: Economy and Space*, 38(10), 1843–61. https://doi.org/10.1068/a37205.

Janarthanan, V. (2012). 'Serious Video Games: Games for Education and Health'. *Ninth International Conference on Information Technology – New Generations*, 875–78. https://doi.org/10.1109/itng.2012.79.

Kain, E. (2019). '"Death Stranding" Shamelessly Bombards You with Corporate Product Placements'. Forbes. www.forbes.com/sites/erikkain/2019/11/09/death-stranding-shamelessly-bombards-you-with-corporate-product-placements/. Accessed 27 September 2021.

Kallio, K. P., Mayra, F., Kaipainen, K. (2011). 'At Least Nine Ways to Play: Approaching Gamer Mentalities'. *Games and Culture,* 6(4), 327–53. https://doi.org/10.1177/1555412010391089.

Keogh, B. (2018). 'From Aggressively Formalised to Intensely in/Formalised: Accounting for a Wider Range of Videogame Development Practices'. *Creative Industries Journal*, 12(1), 14–33. https://doi.org/10.1080/17510694.2018.1532760.

Khatib, F., Cooper, S., Tyka, M. D. et al. (2011). 'Algorithm Discovery by Protein Folding Game Players'. *Proceedings of the National Academy of Sciences*, 108(47). www.pnas.org/content/108/47/18949.short.

Kojima Productions (2019). *Death Stranding*. Sony Interactive Entertainment.

Koops van 't Jagt, R., Hoeks, J. C. J., Dorleijn, G. J. & Hendriks, P. (2014). 'Look Before You Leap: How Enjambment Affects the Processing of Poetry'. *Scientific Study of Literature*, 4(1), 3–24. https://doi.org/10.1075/Ssol.4.1.01jag.

Kultima, A. (2021). 'Game Jam Natives? The Rise of the Game Jam Era in Game Development Cultures'. *ICGJ 2021: Sixth Annual International Conference on Game Jams, Hackathons, and Game Creation Events*. New York: Association for Computing Machinery, 22–28. https://doi.org/10.1145/3472688.3472691.

Langacker, R. W. (2007). 'Cognitive Grammar'. In D. Geeraerts & H. Cuyckens (eds.), *Oxford Handbook of Cognitive Linguistics*. Oxford: Oxford University Press, 421–62.

Langacker, R. W. (2008). *Cognitive Grammar: A Basic Introduction*. New York: Oxford University Press.

Langdell, T. (2006). 'Beware of the Localization'. In C. Bateman (ed.), *Game Writing: Narrative Skills for Videogames*. Hingham: Charles River Media, 201–8.

Larsen, L. J. (2017). 'Play and Gameful Movies: The Ludification of Modern Cinema'. *Games and Culture*, 14(5), 455–77. https://doi.org/10.1177/1555412017700601.

Lieberman, D. A. (2012). 'Video Games for Diabetes Self-Management: Examples and Design Strategies'. *Journal of Diabetes Science and Technology*, 6(4), 802–6. https://doi.org/10.1177/193229681200600410.

Liew, Z. R. & Che Omar, H. (2018). 'Understanding Fansub as One of the Audiovisual Translation Method'. *Kemanusiaan: The Asian Journal of Humanities*, 25(2), 109–27. https://doi.org/10.21315/kajh2018.25.2.6.

Lipkin, N. D. (2019). 'The Indiepocalypse: The Political-Economy of Independent Game Development Labor in Contemporary Indie Markets'. *Game Studies*, 19(2). http://gamestudies.org/1902/articles/lipkin.

Lloyd, B. (2019). 'Yes, There's a LOT of Product Placement in "Death Stranding"'. Entertainment.ie. www.entertainment.ie/gaming/death-stranding-product-placement-428856. Accessed 26 August 2022.

Lörscher, W. (1991). *Translation Performance, Translation Process, and Translation Strategies: A Psycholinguistic Investigation*, vol. 4. Tubingen: Gunter Narr.

Lowood, H. (2021). 'Electronic Game'. *Encyclopaedia Britannica*. 1 November. www.britannica.com/topic/electronic-game. Accessed 17 September 2021.

Lv, Z., Tek, A., Da Silva, F., Empereur-mot, C., Chavent, M. & Baaden, M. (2013). 'Game on, Science – How Video Game Technology May Help Biologists Tackle Visualization Challenges'. *PLoS ONE*, 8(3), Article e57990. https://doi.org/10.1371/journal.pone.0057990.

Maguire, T. (2015). *Accessible Theatre-Making for Spectators with Visual Impairment: Cahoots NI's* The Gift. Belfast: Ulster University.

Mangiron, C. & O'Hagan, M. (2006). 'Game Localisation: Unleashing Imagination with "Restricted" Translation'. *The Journal of Specialised Translation*, 6, 10–21.

Mangiron, C. (2018). 'Reception Studies in Game Localisation: Taking Stock'. In E. Di Giovanni & Y. Gambier (eds.), *Reception Studies and Audiovisual Translation*. Amsterdam: John Benjamins, 277–96.

Massive Entertainment (2017). 'INSIDE MASSIVE – Episode 1: Join the Family'. YouTube video. www.youtu.be/KkGHZjgJfDM/. Accessed 7 September 2021.

Matamala, A. &Orero, P. (2015). 'Text on Screen'. In A. Remael, N. Reviers & G. Vercauteren (eds.), *Pictures Painted in Words: ADLAB Audio Description Guidelines*. ADLAB. www.adlabproject.eu/Docs/adlab%20book/index.html.

Matern, M. F., van der Westhuizen, A. & Mostert, S. N. (2019). 'The Effects of Video Gaming on Visual Selective Attention'. *South African Journal of Psychology*, 1(12), 183–94. https://doi.org/10.1177/0081246319871391.

Missing Mountain (2019). *Eden* [Game]. Missing Mountain. https://missingmountain.itch.io/eden.

Musselwhite, C., Marston, H. R. & Freeman, S. (2016). 'From Needy and Dependent to Independent Homo Ludens: Exploring Digital Gaming and Older People'. *Games and Culture*, 11(1–2), 3–6. https://doi.org/10.1177/1555412015605220.

Nacke, L. E., & Lindley, C. A. (2010). 'Affective Ludology, Flow and Immersion in a First-Person Shooter: Measurement of Player Experience'. *Loading... The Journal of the Canadian Game Studies Association*, 3(5), 1–21. https://doi.org/10.48550/arXiv.1004.0248.

Naishuller, I. (dir.) (2021). *Nobody*. Universal Pictures.

Nallawalla, K. (2019). 'Product Placement in Video Games'. Good/Bad Marketing. www.goodbadmarketing.com/keith/product-placement-in-video-games/.

NAWA (Narodowa Agencja Wymiany Akademickiej – Polish National Agency for Academic Exchange) (2020). 'Poland Is Leading the Way of Gaming Industry. How?' https://study.gov.pl/news/poland-leading-way-gaming-industry-how.

NLS (National Library Service for the Blind and Print Disabled) (2015). 'Video Gaming Accessibility'. www.loc.gov/nls/resources/general-resources-on-disabilities/video-gaming-accessibility/.

O'Hagan, M. (2009). 'Towards a Cross-Cultural Game Design: An Explorative Study in Understanding the Player Experience of a Localised Japanese Video Game'. *The Journal of Specialised Translation*, 11, 211–33.

O'Hagan, M. (2019). 'Game Localization: A Critical Overview and Implications for Audiovisual Translation'. In Luis Pérez-González (ed.), *The Routledge Handbook of Audiovisual Translation*. Abingdon: Routledge, 145–59.

O'Hagan, M. & Mangiron, C. (2013). *Game Localization: Translating for the Global Digital Entertainment Industry*. Amsterdam: John Benjamins.

Palumbo, A. (2018). '"High Likelihood" That Video Game Revenue Will Be 100% Digital by 2022, Says Piper Jaffray'. Wccftech. https://wccftech.com/video-game-revenue-100-digital-by-2022/. Accessed 27 September 2021.

Pan European Gaming Information (2017). 'Statistics about PEGI'. Interactive Software Federation of Europe. https://web.archive.org/web/20180629131125/https://pegi.info/page/statistics-about-pegi. Accessed 27 August 2022.

Pan European Gaming Information (2020). 'Statistics about PEGI'. Interactive Software Federation of Europe. https://pegi.info/page/statistics-about-pegi. Accessed 27 September 2021.

Parini, I. (2015). 'Cultural and Linguistic Issues at Play in the Management of Multilingual Films in Dubbing'. In Ł. Bogucki & M. Deckert (eds.), *Accessing Audiovisual Translation*. Frankfurt: Peter Lang, 27–50.

Patel, F. & Lynch, H. (2013). 'Glocalization as an Alternative to Internationalization in Higher Education: Embedding Positive Glocal Learning Perspectives'. *International Journal of Teaching and Learning in Higher Education*, 25(2), 223–30. https://files.eric.ed.gov/fulltext/EJ1016539.pdf.

Paul, C. A. (2014). 'Meaning'. In M. J. P. Wolf & B. Perron (eds.), *The Routledge Companion to Video Game Studies*. New York: Routledge, 459–65.

Pedersen, J. (2007). 'Scandinavian Subtitles: A Comparative Study of Subtitling Norms in Sweden and Denmark with a Focus on Extralinguistic Cultural References'. Doctoral thesis, Stockholm University.

Peña Pérez Negrón, A., Bonilla Carranza, D., & Berumen Mora, J. (2021). 'Cutting-Edge Technology for Video Games'. In J. Mejia, M. Muñoz, Á. Rocha, & Y. Quiñonez (eds.), *New Perspectives in Software Engineering: CIMPS 2020 – Advances in Intelligent Systems and Computing*, vol. 1297. Cham: Springer, https://doi.org/10.1007/978-3-030-63329-5_20.

Przybylski, A. K., Deci, E. L., Rigby, C. S. & Ryan, R. M. (2014). 'Competence-Impeding Electronic Games and Players' Aggressive Feelings, Thoughts, and Behaviors'. *Journal of Personality and Social Psychology*, 106(3), 441–57. https://doi.org/10.1037/a0034820.

Pursel, B. K. & Stubbs, C. (2017). 'How Multiplayer Video Games Can Help Prepare Individuals for Some of the World's Most Stressful Jobs'. In M. McNeese & P. Forster (eds.), *Cognitive Systems Engineering an Integrative Living Laboratory Framework*, 1st ed. Boca Raton: CRC Press, 277–95.

Rawitsch, D., Heinemann, B. & Dillenberger, P. (1971). *The Oregon Trail* [Game]. MECC.

Reiss, K. (2000). *Translation Criticism – The Potentials & Limitation: Categories and Criteria for Translation Quality Assessment*. Manchester: St Jerome.

Rock, I., Linnet, C. M., Grant, P. I. & Mack, A. (1992). 'Perception without Attention: Results of a New Method'. *Cognitive Psychology*, 24(4), 502–34.

Rocksteady Studios (2011). *Batman: Arkham City* [Game]. Warner Bros.

Romero-Fresco, P. (2013). 'Accessible Filmmaking: Joining the Dots between Audiovisual Translation, Accessibility and Filmmaking'. *Journal of Specialised Translation*, 20, 201–23. www.jostrans.org/issue20/art_romero.php.

Romero-Fresco, P. (2019). 'Accessible Filmmaking: Integrating Translation and Accessibility into the Filmmaking Process'. London: Routledge.

Romero-Fresco, P. (2020) 'Accessible Filmmaking'. In Ł. Bogucki and M. Deckert (eds.), *The Palgrave Handbook of Audiovisual Translation and Media Accessibility*. London: Palgrave, 545–66.

Sanford, K., Starr, L. J., Merkel, L., & Bonsor Kurki, S. (2015). 'Serious Games: Video Games for Good?' *E-Learning and Digital Media*, 12(1), 90–106. https://doi.org/10.1177/2042753014558380.

Sapkowski, A. (1986). *Wiedźmin* [Witcher] series. Poland: Supernowa.

'ScanTek' (n.d.). The Division Wiki. https://thedivision.fandom.com/wiki/Contact_Lens. Accessed 4 September 2021.

'Shadow Warrior 2' (n.d.). How Long to Beat. https://howlongtobeat.com/game.php?id=39740. Accessed 14 August 2020.

Shaffer, D. W., Squire, K. R., Halverson, R., & Gee, J. P. (2005). 'Video Games and the Future of Learning'. *Phi Delta Kappan*, 87(2), 105–11. https://doi.org/10.1177/003172170508700205.

Simons, J. & Rensink, R. (2005). 'Change Blindness: Past, Present, and Future'. *Trends in Cognitive Sciences* 9(1), 16–20.

Slade, D. (2018). *Black Mirror: Bandersnatch*. Netflix.

Sperber, D. & Wilson, D. (1995). *Relevance: Communication and Cognition*, 2nd ed. Oxford: Blackwell.

Sternheimer, K. (2007). 'Do Video Games Kill?' *Contexts*, 6(1), 13–17. https://doi.org/10.1525/ctx.2007.6.1.13.

'Strategic Homeland Division' (n.d.). The Division Wiki. https://thedivision.fandom.com/wiki/Strategic_Homeland_Division. Accessed 16 September 2020.

Suellentrop, C. (2017). '"Witcher" Studio Boss Marcin Iwinski: "We Had No Clue How to Make Games"'. *Rolling* Stone. March 15. https://web.archive.org/web/20170802203720/www.rollingstone.com/glixel/interviews/witcher-studio-boss-we-had-no-clue-how-to-make-games-w472316/. Accessed 27 August 2022.

Suojanen, T., Koskinen, K. & Tuominen, T. (2015). *User-Centered Translation*. London: Routledge.

Team Silent (2001). *Silent Hill 2* [Game]. Konami.

'Tom Clancy's The Division' (n.d.). Game Lengths. www.gamelengths.com/games/playtimes/Tom+Clancy's+The+Division/. Accessed 14 August 2020.

'Tom Clancy's The Division 2' (n.d.). How Long to Beat. https://howlongtobeat.com/game?id=57480. Accessed 14 August 2020.

Telltale Games (2009). *Sam and Max Save the World* [Game]. Telltale Games.

Tomlin, R. S. & Myachykov, A. (2015). 'Attention and Salience'. In E. Dąbrowska & D. Divjak (eds.), *Handbook of Cognitive Linguistics*. Berlin: De Gruyter, 31–52.

Tondello, G. F., Wehbe R. R., Orji R., Ribeiro, G. & Nacke, L. E. (2017). 'A Framework and Taxonomy of Videogame Playing Preferences'. In: *CHI PLAY '17: Proceedings of the Annual Symposium on Computer-Human Interaction in Play*. New York: Association for Computing Machinery, 329–40. https://doi.org/10.1145/3116595.3116629.

Turel, O. (2020). 'Videogames and Guns in Adolescents: Tests of a Bipartite Theory'. *Computers in Human Behavior*, 109, Article 106355. https://doi.org/10.1016/j.chb.2020.106355.

Turel, O. & Bechara, A. (2019). 'Little Video-Gaming in Adolescents Can Be Protective, but Too Much is Associated with Increased Substance Use'. *Substance Use & Misuse*, 54(3), 384–95. https://doi.org/10.1080/10826084.2018.1496455.

Tyler, J. & Howarth, L. (1983). *Adventure Programs*. London: Usborne.

Ubisoft & Ubisoft Montreal (2015). *Tom Clancy's Rainbow Six: Siege* [Game]. Ubisoft.

Ubisoft, Red Storm Entertainment & Massive Entertainment (2019). *Tom Clancy's The Division 2* [Game]. Ubisoft.

Unity Technologies (n.d.). 'Class LocalizeStringEvent'. Unity Technologies Scripting API. https://docs.unity3d.com/Packages/com.unity.localization@0.7/api/UnityEngine.Localization.Components.LocalizeStringEvent.html. Accessed 17 September 2021.

Uysal, D. (2017). 'Bilgisayar oyunlarinda bağimlilik, şiddet ve kimlik kaybinin çocuk ve gençler üzerindeki etkileri: Burkhard Spinnen'in "Nevena" adli romani [Effects of Addiction, Violence and Loss of Identity in Computer Games on Lives of Children and Young People: Burkhard Spinnen's Novel 'Nevena']'. *Journal of Academic Social Science Studies* (56), 177–200. http://dx.doi.org/10.9761/JASSS7005.

Valve (2007–11). *Portal* series [Games]. Valve.

Valve (2007). *Team Fortress 2* [Game]. Valve.

Vitka, W. (2019). 'How The Division 2 Video Game Recreated and Destroyed DC'. WTOP. https://wtop.com/entertainment/2019/03/washington-wasteland-how-one-of-the-years-biggest-video-games-recreated-and-destroyed-dc/.

Wahl, C. (2008). 'Du Deutscher, Toi Français, You English: Beautiful! – The Polyglot Film as a Genre'. In M. Christensen & N. Erdŏgan (eds.), *Shifting Landscapes: Film and Media in European Context*. Newcastle: Cambridge Scholars Publishing, 334–50.

Whaley, B. (2015). '"Who Will Play Terebi Gemu When No Japanese Children Remain?" Distanced Engagement in Atlus' Catherine'. *Games and Culture*, 13(1), 92–114. https://doi.org/10.1177/1555412015606533.

William, J. (1890/1950). *The Principles of Psychology*. New York: Dover Publications.

Wolf, M. J. P. & Perron, B. (2003). *The Video Game Theory Reader*. New York: Routledge.

Wong, H. (2011). 'A Study of the Video Game Industry in US Metropolitan Areas Using Occupational Analysis'. Master's thesis, University of Massachusetts.

Young, C. J. (2018). 'Game Changers: Everyday Gamemakers and the Development of the Video Game Industry'. Doctoral thesis, University of Toronto.

Zanotti, S. (2018). 'Auteur Dubbing: Translation, Performance and Authorial Control in the Dubbed Versions of Stanley Kubrick's Films'. In I. Ranzato & S. Zanotti (eds.), *Reassessing Dubbing: The Past is Present*. Amsterdam: John Benjamins.

Zhang, L. & Weisi, L. (2013). *Selective Visual Attention: Computational Models and Applications*. Singapore: John Wiley.

Acknowledgements

Research conducted as part of the project 'Visual-Verbal Stimuli in Video Games: A Translation Perspective' under the Excellence Initiative – Research University (IDUB) programme at the University of Lodz. We also extend our gratitude for insights and support to Michał Mazur of Flying Wild Hog as well as to Karolina Majer and Kamil Ściana of Ubisoft Poland.

Cambridge Elements ☰

Translation and Interpreting

Kirsten Malmkjær
University of Leicester

Kirsten Malmkjær is Professor Emeritus of Translation Studies at the University of Leicester. She has taught Translation Studies at the universities of Birmingham, Cambridge, Middlesex and Leicester and has written extensively on aspects of both the theory and practice of the discipline. *Translation and Creativity* (London: Routledge) was published in 2020 and *The Cambridge Handbook of Translation*, which she edited, was published in 2022. She is preparing a volume entitled *Introducing Translation* for the Cambridge Introductions to Language and Linguistics series.

Sabine Braun
University of Surrey

Sabine Braun is Professor of Translation Studies and Director of the Centre for Translation Studies at the University of Surrey. She is a world-leading expert on interpreting and on research into human and machine interaction in translation and interpreting, and holds an Expanding Excellence in England grant to investigate technology-assisted methods, modalities and socio-technological practices of translation and interpreting. She has written extensively on the theory and practice of interpreting, including *Videoconference and Remote Interpreting in Criminal Proceedings*, with J. Taylor, (2012); *Here or There: Research on Interpreting via Video Link*, with J. Napier and R. Skinner (2018). She is editing *Innovation in Audio Description Research*, with K. Starr (2019), and guest-editing a special issue of the *Interpreter and Translator Trainer* with Russo (2020). She is a member of the AHRC Peer Review College.

About the Series
Elements in Translation and Interpreting present cutting-edge studies on the theory, practice and pedagogy of translation and interpreting. The series also features work on machine learning and AI, and human-machine interaction, exploring how they relate to multilingual societies with varying communication and accessibility needs, as well as text-focused research.

Cambridge Elements ☰

Translation and Interpreting

Elements in the Series

Translation and Genre
B. J. Woodstein

Translation as Experimentalism
Tong King Lee

On-Screen Language in Video Games
Mikołaj Deckert and Krzysztof Hejduk

A full series listing is available at: www.cambridge.org/EITI

9 781009 045513